HOW TO
EARN $30,000
A MONTH PLAYING
ONLINE POKER

HOW TO
EARN $30,000
A MONTH PLAYING
ONLINE POKER

OR, THE DEFINITIVE GUIDE TO NO-LIMIT
SINGLE TABLE TOURNAMENTS ONLINE

RYAN WISEMAN

ECW Press

Published by ECW Press
2120 Queen Street East, Suite 200
Toronto, Ontario, Canada M4E 1E2
416.694.3348 / info@ecwpress.com

LIBRARY AND ARCHIVES CANADA CATALOGUING IN PUBLICATION

Wiseman, Ryan
Earn $30,000 per month playing online poker : a step-by-step guide to single table
tournaments / Ryan Wiseman.

ISBN 978-1-55022-788-8

1. Poker. 2. Internet gambling. 3. Gambling systems. I. Title. II. Title: Earn thirty
thousand dollars per month playing online poker.

GV1251.W58 2007   795.412   C2007-903486-1

Cover and text design: Tania Craan
Typesetting: Gail Nina
Production: Rachel Brooks
Second Printing: Thomson-Shore

PRINTED AND BOUND IN THE UNITED STATES

ECW PRESS
ecwpress.com

TABLE OF CONTENTS

♥   PART THREE   ♥

♦   PART FOUR   ♦

INTRODUCTION

Much like a pilot need not know the pure physics behind a flight, a skilled poker player need not know the pure mathematics behind winning poker play. Too often poker books have taken a purely theoretical approach to poker instruction. They present the reader with a flood of mathematical proofs, complex scenarios, and tiresome examples — all of which overwhelm the beginner. Indeed, *we* were once overwhelmed by these books, confused over how anyone could absorb the knowledge therein without a PhD in statistical analysis. How could one person possibly retain, then efficiently apply, all of the information in these books without months of study? Where was the step-by-step approach to defeating online poker?

We began playing online poker in 2003. We were full-time university students and part-time fish. There is no denying the fact that we were all losing players back then. We went online to gamble, and it showed. It was only a matter of time before one of us stood up and said, "I don't want to lose anymore." So he read a few books, found them confusing, but studied hard. By 2004, he was no longer a losing player. In fact, he was a consistent winner. That year he forfeited summer employment to play poker full time, and by the start of the next academic year he was earning significantly more than the rest of us. What was our response? Teach us!

Over the next few months, we observed our friend constantly. The learning process quickly became addictive as each day took us closer to financial freedom. Our friend had read seven poker books that summer. Over 2,500 pages of tedious, technical reading. He said that, for every 50 pages he'd read, only one had contributed to his success. He had photocopied the key pages and kept them in a stapled pile next to his computer — 2,500 pages condensed to a 50-page reference package.

By the end of 2004, we were all winning players. All of us contributed to each other's success, feeding off the combined body of experiential knowledge we had collectively acquired. We played at over 30 different online poker sites, at every limit available (at the time). Eventually, however, *we all settled on one type of game: the no-limit Texas Hold'em sit-'n'-go (single table) tournament.*

Initially, we chose to specialize in the no-limit sit-'n'-go (or NL-SNG) tournaments because it helped to structure our playing time. As students, we needed to be able to walk away from poker at specific times. SNGs have very predictable durations (40–60 minutes), so we could effectively set aside blocks of time to play. However, it quickly became apparent that they offered further advantages. Unlike other games, SNGs had very predictable win/loss rates, could be defeated systematically, and offered an innate system of progression. That is, the various buy-in amounts can be viewed as a ladder that helps us to gauge our success.

Just six months into 2005, we had each earned in excess of $100,000 U.S., and only one of us actually understood the math behind our winning play. The rest of us? Well, we were more than content in our ignorance.

Invariably, other friends became curious about our success. They wanted to know how they could replicate our earnings. While the method we were using was extremely straightforward, we simply did not have the time to teach each person individually. They asked if there was a specific book they should read. The answer was always no, though we wished there was! Eventually, one of us wrote a brief paper explaining how to defeat the low-limit SNGs at PartyPoker. It provided the reader with *only the information required to beat that spe-*

cific low-limit. We gave it to someone every time they asked for poker lessons, and everyone seemed to succeed. It was then that we had our epiphany: we could write a step-by-step guide to defeating SNGs. A book that provides the reader with information on a need-to-know basis. A book that can show a beginner how to turn a very small initial investment into hundreds of thousands of dollars. A book based on experience. This is the result of that epiphany.

What we have created is unique. It is the only poker book available that caters specifically to online SNG tournaments. More importantly, it's the only poker book that guides the reader on a progressive path upward through the various limits. We don't waste time with information irrelevant to your current limit. We provide you with only the information necessary to win with your current bankroll and/or skill level. Presented in a series of steps, our book outlines your goals, providing guidelines that help you to tell when you are ready to move on. This is the book we wished we had when we were beginning. That being said, it's also the book we wished we had when we were succeeding! It began as a guide to help friends. Now it's a guide to help the masses.

While this book begins with the assumption that the reader has no knowledge of SNG tournaments, we do expect the reader to have a basic understanding of both poker and, specifically, Texas Hold'em. The following concepts should be understood before you begin.

- You should understand poker hand rankings (royal flush, straight flush, flush, etc.).
- You should understand how Texas Hold'em is played (general rules, how it's dealt).

We decided to omit this information from the book since most readers will likely already have it engrained. Additionally, the information is available so readily elsewhere that it seemed excessive to include it in this book. However, should you be unfamiliar with these general concepts, or wish to refresh your memory, please visit the following websites.

- General poker review:
http://www.partypoker.com/how_to_play/.

- Hand rankings:
http://www.partypoker.com/how_to_play/poker_school/
basic_poker_rules/rank_of_hands.html

- Texas Hold'em overview:
http://www.partypoker.com/how_to_play/poker_school/
poker_games/texas_holdem.html.

- Texas Hold'em downloadable guide:
http://www.partypoker.com/images/docs/holdem.pdf.

These websites will provide you with an overview of most basic poker concepts, including information related to PartyPoker's software (the software we'll be using). Additionally, should you encounter any confusion related to terminology used in this book, please refer to the glossary.

♠ PART ONE ♠
An Overview

How to Use This Book

While we recommend that anyone unfamiliar with online poker, and specifically SNG tournaments, read this book in its entirety, we haven't designed it to be tedious and redundant for the more experienced player. Ultimately, this book should be used as a dependable resource and source of reference. We encourage you to mark memorable pages and skim over passages dealing with familiar concepts.

A Beginner's Guide to Online Poker

It's estimated that the online poker industry currently generates gross revenues in excess of $2 billion per year. Gone are the days when shady Internet sites lured the occasional customer into their midst only to exploit them through complex cash-out procedures, flawed software, and untouchable customer support. Modern online poker sites can more appropriately be viewed as corporations (many are corporately owned) that are held accountable for their actions and that recognize their success depends on their customers' enjoyment.

Many people new to online poker wonder how these sites can generate such incredible amounts of revenue. The roots of their profits are the same as land-based poker rooms: *rake*. Poker sites scoop a predetermined percentage (the rake) from every pot above a certain amount. These amounts vary per game and per limit. Since the focus of our book is on tournaments, it's important to understand how the house (poker site) makes money from tournaments.

For every tournament played, a fee is charged by the poker site. For example, if you enter an $11 tournament with 10 players, the total amount everyone puts in is $110. However, the prize pool is only $100. You are actually entering a $10 tournament and providing the house with a dollar to let you play. This is an unavoidable side effect of playing poker *anywhere*. Everyone has to pay it, and it will not impede your success. Tournament fees will be covered in greater detail later in this book.

The poker site we'll be studying throughout this book is PartyPoker. It's the largest online poker site, regularly hosting 85,000 players at a time. This number guarantees there will be action at any limit at which you desire to play. PartyPoker also hosts the greatest number of SNG tournaments. Since SNGs are the topic of this book, we believe it's important to learn how to beat the tournaments where most people are playing. Not only are the games easier (since with an increased number of players comes an increased number of *bad* players), but they also have a tournament format that is relatively similar to many of the other online poker sites. Feel free to experiment with other poker sites, taking what you have learned here and applying it elsewhere. We have included simple conversion tables at the end of the book (Part 4) that allow you to easily apply the method described here to other popular poker sites. It's our belief and experience, however, that PartyPoker offers the most lucrative games on the Internet.

In addition to the quality of the games, PartyPoker supports a variety of cash-out methods and offers 100% secure and guaranteed transactions. You can remain confident that your money is secure within your account.

Opening an Online Poker Account

(If you already have a PartyPoker account, please skip this section.)

Many people have been tempted to make the move to online poker but have seen the task of setting up an online account as daunting. We assure you that there's nothing more to it than signing in to an e-mail account or banking online.

Visit www.sngprofessional.com. This is the companion website for this book. Here you'll find a download link and step-by-step instructions on how to install PartyPoker's software. Signing up through our site permits us to anonymously track the progress of our readers. Anonymous statistics are sent to us through PartyPoker's affiliate program. It's important that we mention PartyPoker is in no way associated with the creation or publication of this book. The statistics provided to us show how our readers are doing as a group; no individual information is provided. We will try and make this information public monthly to see just how well all of us are doing. If you choose not to sign up through our affiliate, we completely understand. We don't make our money through sign-ups. To sign up independently, visit www.partypoker.com. You'll see a download link on the main page. Simply click on it and install the software.

Once the software has been installed and loaded, follow the step-by-step instructions provided and sign up with PartyPoker. Any problem or confusion can be addressed by contacting PartyPoker at 1-800-852-4719 or by visiting its website.

Once you have opened your account, it's time to make your first deposit. There are various methods of deposit available to you. Again, full details of these methods can be found on PartyPoker's website. We will, however, offer a few quick suggestions.

> **1.** Credit card deposits are the easiest and most straightforward method. However, you can't withdraw to your credit card. Be prepared to withdraw via check if you choose this method.

2. Neteller: www.neteller.com. If you plan on being involved with online poker for some time, we recommend signing up for a Neteller account. This is essentially an online bank account. You can link it to your personal bank account and deposit to or withdraw from that account. Withdrawals from PartyPoker to Neteller are almost instantaneous. (*Note: As of summer 2007, Neteller is no longer available to North American customers. Europeans can still use it at will.*)

The amount you deposit is completely up to you. Remember, you can withdraw or deposit more funds at will. Bankroll requirements will be discussed prior to play. We simply recommend depositing a small amount now to eliminate any confusion that may arise later. Doing so will also give you practice using the software while you finish this book.

Familiarize yourself with the software. We encourage you to visit http://www.partypoker.com/how_to_play/. Become accustomed to the various menus and features. While all of this will soon become second nature to you, it's important to alleviate any confusion prior to playing.

Configuring PartyPoker's Software for Tournaments

To take advantage of the additional software we recommend you use when playing PartyPoker's tournaments (discussed later), you should configure PartyPoker so that it displays only the minimum required graphics. Under "Game Rules & Options," go to "Video & Audio Options." We recommend unchecking all options except "Mouse Over Help." Doing so will also reduce your system requirements and increase the visual speed of the game.

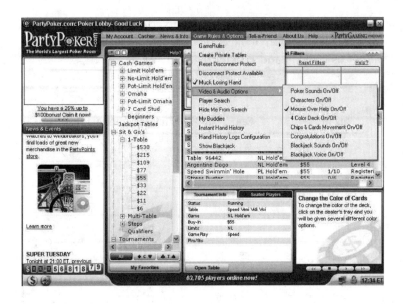

PartyPoker's SNG Tournament Structure

(See Part 4 for tournament structure charts that relate to other poker sites.)

The structure of a single-table tournament is not unlike that of any other 10-person table game you have ever played. There exists both a small blind (SB) and a big blind (BB), along with a dealer button. Unlike table games, however, everyone sitting at the SNG table has a predetermined amount of chips (2,000 for all of PartyPoker's tournaments). You are unable to buy more chips if you lose some, and once you lose all of your chips you are out of the tournament. It continues until only one person remains.

It's important to understand the structure of these tournaments prior to playing them since it holds the key to your outcome. Here we examine the SNG format we'll focus on: 10-player no-limit single-table tournaments.

Buy-in amounts: PartyPoker offers a variety of limits at which to play SNGs. Our book is designed to help you climb this ladder as quickly and efficiently as possible.

Buy-In	Fee	Total Tournament Cost
$5	$1	$6
$10	$1	$11
$20	$2	$22
$30	$3	$33
$50	$5	$55
$70	$7	$77
$100	$9	$109
$200	$15	$215
$500	$30	$530

Pay-out structure: The prize pool consists of each player's tournament buy-in. The tournament fee is not included in the prize pool. As you can see above, an $11 tournament ($10 + $1) yields a prize pool of $100 (not $111). For PartyPoker SNGs, the pay-out structure is as follows.

First place	50% of prize pool
Second place	30% of prize pool
Third place	20% of prize pool

Blinds' structure: The blinds are the most important element of the game. Without a solid understanding of blind structure, you won't be able to time and manage your bets. Each blind level lasts for a predetermined amount of time, then moves up to the next level. The blinds start as a small percentage of your chip stack, then increase as time goes on. Regular SNGs have 10-minute levels: that is, the levels increase every ten minutes, while Speed SNGs have five-minute levels.

Level	SB	BB	Ante
1	20	40	-
2	30	60	-
3	50	100	-
4	100	200	-
5	200	400	-
6	300	600	-
7	400	800	25
8	600	1,200	50
9	1,000	2,000	75
10	1,500	3,000	75

Don't be overly concerned with memorizing each level; it's simply a good idea to have an overview of the tournament structure. The importance of each level will be explained later.

Information regarding the current level, and the time until the next level, is always available to you in the bottom left-hand corner of each table.

The Two Tournament Types: Speed versus Regular

PartyPoker offers two types of SNG tournaments: Speed and Regular. They differ in only one way: *the length of each blind level.*

> *Speed*: Each blind level lasts five minutes.
> *Regular*: Each blind level lasts 10 minutes.

Each tournament type has its advantages and disadvantages. Speed takes less time to complete but permits you to see fewer hands per level. Regular tournaments take twice as long to complete but permit a more patient and less variable game. Our method will teach you how to defeat both types of tournaments, and we will discuss each type in much greater detail later in the book. Ultimately, however, we recommend you choose a tournament type and stick with it once you have had a chance to experience both.

The Tools of the Trade

Software to Help You Win

Now that you have set up your poker account, and PartyPoker is properly installed, you need to set up the tools necessary for success. It's important that these components are in place before you begin to play. While the lower limits of play are easily beaten without them, we recommend you set everything up now so you are fully familiar with them when you progress to higher limits (where they are absolutely necessary).

Unlike land-based poker, online poker provides you with a variety of technological advantages that can enhance your ability to interpret opponents. Software has also been created to help manage PartyPoker more effectively and increase the ease with which you can play multiple tables at once. We will present the tools in their order of necessity.

POKER TRACKER: www.pokertracker.com ($55 U.S.)

It's highly recommended that you download Poker Tracker. Unfortunately, the only way to acquire it is to purchase it from the website, but the whole process takes no more than five minutes. You'll be able to download and use it immediately. If you wish to continue without using Poker Tracker, your progress will be slower.

Poker Tracker, in its simplest form, is a database management tool. It keeps track of every tournament and hand played, then interprets and presents the data in a straightforward manner. It provides us with information directly related to both our, and our opponents', progress and playing styles. In the context of this book, Poker Tracker will primarily be used as a tool that helps us to better understand our opponents. Poker Tracker has many features, so we'll focus only on those that benefit our purpose: defeating SNG tournaments.

The first time you run Poker Tracker, it will walk you through the general setup procedure. Once this is complete, the software is fully operational.

For every tournament we play, we set Poker Tracker to automatically import all the hands played and thus track every player we play against. There are two ways to do this: one provides you with live updates while you play; the other updates stats once the tournament is over. We will go over both of them, and you can select which method you find most efficient; we recommend using both.

- Importing Hand Histories as You Play

Stats are constantly being updated as you play. Every few minutes Poker Tracker imports new data, presenting you with the most up-to-date player information available. The setup procedure is straightforward.

> In Poker Tracker, click on "Auto-Import Hand Histories/Tournament Summaries — Generic Setup." The following window will pop up.

The "Use:" selection box should read "Look for a file (or files) on my PC." The timer should be set to five minutes. The "All Text Files In Folder (sub-folders included)" option should be clicked. Under the "Folder(s) where hand history files are located:" you should have the location of the PartyPoker hand history folder. The default is shown above; however, you may have to enter something different if you installed PartyPoker elsewhere. You can alter the folder location by clicking on the "Configure…" button.

Once this is set, simply click on "OK." You will now be presented with the following window.

```
H  Auto-Import Hand Histories/Tournament Summaries          [_][□][X]
Database: ap                                                    Help
☐ Enable logging (use this only if instructed by Poker Tracker support).
☐ Move processed files to the following folder when I close this window:
  [                                                    ]  Browse...
☐ Auto rate players when importing hand histories (ring hands only).
[ Configure Import of Observed Hands (Party & Affiliates only)... ]
[   Stop Timer   ]  [   Force Import   ]  [  Change Settings  ]  ☐ Hide status window
Status:  [c][p]  Timer fires in 297 seconds
┌───────────────────────────────────────────────────────────┐
│ Timer started...05/23/2006 04:38:07 PM                      │
│                                                             │
│                                                             │
│                                                             │
│                                                             │
│                                                             │
│                                                             │
└───────────────────────────────────────────────────────────┘
```

Poker Tracker is now ready to start importing hand information. You may minimize the software, and it will work in the background. Every five minutes it will check whether or not new hands have been played; if new hands are available, it will import them. Once you are done playing, simply open Poker Tracker and stop the import timer. You may then explore all of the information that was imported by clicking on the "Tournament Player Statistics" icon.

Remember to always start the auto-import process prior to

playing. Doing so will ensure that you have a complete record of all hands played.

Poker Tracker only imports hands if they are available! Don't expect it to find any new hands if you haven't played any new tournaments.

• Importing Hand Histories from E-Mail

Using e-mail for importation has one great advantage over live import: it provides you with the results of your opponents (what places they came in after you left). Live import stops recording once you get kicked out of a tournament, so you never know the final results.

Live import is much more important for the beginner. Ideally, however, you will use both methods. Poker Tracker automatically detects duplicate hands, so you do have to worry about receiving inaccurate results when using both methods at once.

The first requirement for this method is that you have a POP3 e-mail account (not a web-based e-mail account such as Hotmail). These e-mail accounts allow you to use software such as Outlook. You may already have a POP3 account. If you do, you can disregard this step. If you don't already have one, you can acquire a free POP3 account from numerous sites on the Internet, including www.gmail.com or www.bluebottle.com. Both services allow you to check your e-mail online and via e-mail software.

Now you must make sure that your POP3 e-mail account is associated with PartyPoker (this will be the primary e-mail address PartyPoker uses to contact you). Under the "My Account" menu in the PartyPoker lobby, click on "Change/Validate E-mail Address." The following window will pop up.

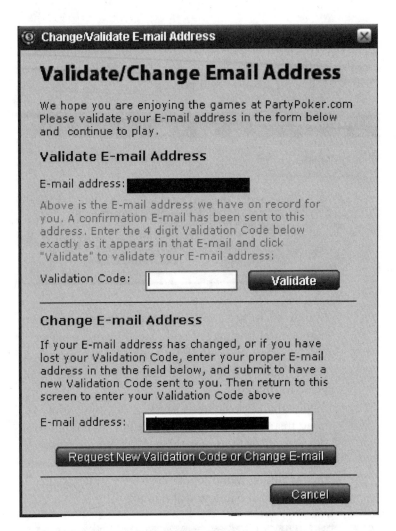

Simply enter your POP3 e-mail address in the "Change E-mail Address" box, request a new validation code, and then check your POP3 e-mail. Once you receive the code, go back into PartyPoker and enter the validation code above and click "Validate." Your POP3 e-mail account is now linked to your PartyPoker account.

To receive hand histories from PartyPoker, you

must request them at the end of every tournament. When you have finished playing any tournament (either by winning it or by getting knocked out), the following window will pop up.

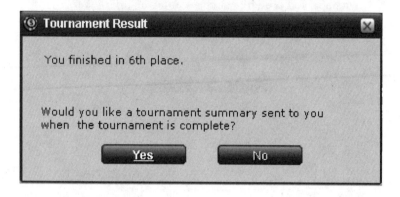

Simply click "Yes," and a complete tournament summary containing every hand played by every player will be sent to your POP3 e-mail account. You should make it a habit of clicking "Yes" at the end of every tournament.

Now that PartyPoker is sending you all of your hand histories, we will show you how to configure Poker Tracker to import them. First, you must configure your e-mail address with Poker Tracker. Under the "Utilities" menu, click on "POP3 Email Setup." The following window will pop up.

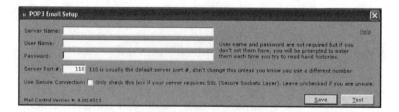

Enter all of your e-mail information into provided boxes; then click "Test." Make sure that it connects, and click "Save."

Now, whenever you want Poker Tracker to import new hand histories, simply click on "Import Hand Histories/Tournament Summaries" under the "File" menu. The following window will pop up.

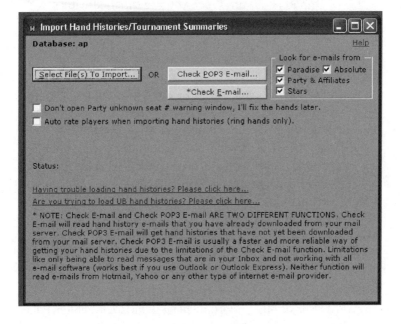

Simply click on "Check POP3 E-mail…," and Poker Tracker will automatically connect to your e-mail account and extract all of the tournament summary e-mails that PartyPoker has sent.

It will then provide you with the following options.

You can instruct Poker Tracker to delete the e-mails once imported if you wish. Doing so will free space in your e-mail account. Make sure that all of the e-mails have a check-mark beside them under the "Import" column. Once you are satisfied with the options, click "Import," and Poker Tracker does the rest. You should make a habit of importing hand histories into Poker Tracker at the end of every poker session.

Once the hand histories are imported, feel free to explore the software and the data that have been imported. We encourage you to look at Poker Tracker in more depth than we have covered here. There is an excellent forum on the website should you need assistance. We have discussed only what is necessary for our SNG method.

POKER-ACE HUD: www.pokeracesoftware.com **($25 U.S.)**
Poker-Ace HUD (heads-up display) works in combination with Poker Tracker. It won't work without a functioning Poker Tracker database.

PAHUD positions important player statistics (which Poker Tracker has collected about your opponents) directly around their names at the poker table. It automatically updates those statistics as you play the tournament, thus giving you a real-time "read" on your opponent.

PAHUD permits you to play multiple tables at the same time without paying attention to how your opponents are playing. All the information you require is directly on the table.

As with Poker Tracker, we will set up PAHUD in a manner specialized for SNG tournaments. Once the PAHUD layout has been set, you'll never have to alter it again.

• Setting Up PAHUD for Tournaments

   1. Once PAHUD is loaded, click on the "Options" menu and select "Layout Manager."

2. Make sure that the "Poker Site" option is set to "Party Poker & Skins" and that the "Table Type" is "10 max."

PokerAce Hud - Layout Manager

File   Edit   Options   Help

Poker Site: | Party Poker & Skins ▼ | Table Type: | 10 max ▼ |

3. We will now remove the stats that you don't need.

• Under the "Stat" menu, select "(Player) Total Aggression Postflop."
• Uncheck the "Visible" box. Doing so will remove this stat from the table.

Stat

| (Player) Total Aggression Postflop ▼ | ☐ Visible
                                             ☐ Show Mine

Formatting

Remove the following stats as well by following the same procedure as above.

• "(Table Avg) Voluntarily Put $ In Pot"
• "(Table Avg) Preflop Raise"
• "(Table Avg) Pot Size"

Before   After

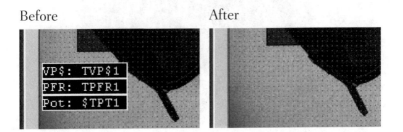

4. Each player seat will now look like this.

At this point, we will add additional stats necessary for tournament play.

- Under "Stat" select "(Player) Continuation Bet."
- Check the "Visible" box to activate the stat.
- You will see a black box titled "CB10" appear in the middle of the screen. The 10 represents the seat number. Click and drag the "CB10" box to the corresponding seat.

• You will notice that there is now a box titled "CB9" in the middle of the table. Position this box on seat nine. Follow this procedure until all boxes are situated in their corresponding seats.

5. Follow the same steps to add all of the following stats to each player as well.

• "(Player) Folded Small Blind to Steal"
• "(Player) Folded Big Blind to Steal"
• "(Player) Attempted to Steal"

Try to arrange the stats in a consistent manner. Consider following our example below.

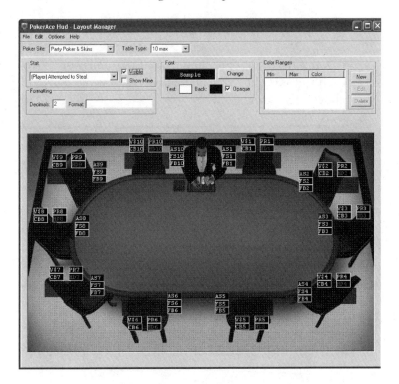

Here is a closer look.

These should be all the stats you need to start. We will incorporate other stats as we progress.

6. Go to the "File" menu and click on "Save."

7. Close the "Layout Manager."

8. Consider creating a simple chart that tells you what each stat is. Doing so will make it easier while playing. Here is an example.

Voluntarily Put $ in Pot (%)	Preflop Raise (%)	Attempt to Steal Blinds (%)
Continuation Bet (%)	Total Hands	Folded SB to Steal (%)
PLAYER 10		Folded BB to Steal (%)

• Setting Up PAHUD Preferences

1. Under the "Options" menu, click on "Preferences."

2. Click on "Filters" in the menu at left.

3. Under "Player Ranges," click on the number there and press "Delete." You should have nothing under both the "Min" and the "Max" columns.

4. Click on "New" and enter each of the following number combinations in order.

Min	Max
7	10
5	7
3	5
2	3

5. The "Filters" page should now look like this.

6. Under the "Poker Sites" menu, click on "Party & Skins." Make sure that the location to which PartyPoker was installed on your system is listed. If not, then use "Add" for its installation location. (All of the default locations are added, so you shouldn't have to add anything.)

7. Click "OK."

Configuring the "Player Ranges" in this way instructs PAHUD to display stats specific to the number of players at the table. In tournaments, the number of players at the table and (related to this) the level the tournament is at drastically alter play. These player ranges help to increase the accuracy of the displayed statistics.

PAHUD is now properly configured. Each time you want to use it, simply load and minimize it.

SNG POWER TOOLS: http://sitngo-analyzer.com (FREE TO TRY, $79 U.S. TO BUY)
SNG Power Tools (SNGPT) is a piece of software that helps you to determine the expected value (EV) of an "all-in" push during a tournament. Essentially, it tells you whether or not the long-term outcome of pushing two specific cards against specific players is a positive one. This software is of little consequence to you right now, but we recommend downloading it anyway. Feel free to play around with it or read up on it. SNGPT will be used once we begin playing.

MULTI-TABLE HELPER: www.multitablehelper.com ($79 U.S.)
MTH is an optional piece of software that may ease some stresses brought about by playing multiple tables at the same time (which you all will be doing soon!). It's relatively inexpensive at $25 and includes unlimited updates for life. Some of the features include

- customized table organization;
- automatic table movement (brings active table to the forefront);

- keyboard-only controls; and
- voice-driven controls.

The most convenient feature of the software is the "SNG Opener." As implied, it automatically opens SNG tournaments for you in the limit, type, and amount of your request. The frustration saved is worth the price alone, as you will eventually find out. Nonetheless, this is merely a luxury, and many people play without this software.

PARTY PLANNER: http://www.overcards.com/wiki/moin.cgi/
PartyPlanner
Party Planner is a free piece of software that shares many of the same features as MTH in regard to table organization. It allows you to instruct where each of your tables opens and the order in which they open. It makes playing more than four tables much easier and is especially beneficial for those of us using two monitors. We recommend that you give it a try if you are experiencing difficulty organizing multiple tables.

POKER MODS (www.pokermods.com)
Poker Mods (modifications) allow the user to alter the graphical appearance of poker tables. You can download new table graphics that may be easier on the eyes or better suit your mood. They are all free to download and are very easy to install.

Hardware to Help You Win
Consider these recommendations optional for the first few tournament levels you progress through. Ultimately, however, you will want to reinvest some of your earnings into a poker-friendly hardware setup that is more conducive to the necessities of play.

The most beneficial hardware investment is the purchase of a second monitor and a video card that permits you to use two monitors at the same time. You can extend your desktop area, thus permitting more tables to be opened at one time without any overlap. We hesitate to suggest brands and prices since these elements fluctuate so frequently. Nonetheless, if you are considering purchasing another monitor for poker, make sure it's no less than a 19" LCD. Consult your local computer shop about the best video card for your needs, though a basic dual-output card should cost no more than $100.

For proof of the benefits of good hardware setups, take a look at the following image.

As you can see, two monitors allow you to dramatically increase desktop space, permitting you to play more tables, at a larger size, with less overlap. The size of the tables can be altered. However, it's advisable to keep the tables as large as possible to reduce both visual and mental strain.

Because PartyPoker's software requires very little computing power to operate smoothly, the only hardware upgrades you'll ever require relate to comfort. Creating a user-friendly, comfortable working environment certainly contributes to success. Common hardware upgrades other than monitor/video changes include a wireless mouse and keyboard, wall-mounting units for monitors, and a high-quality desk chair.

What Is a Bankroll, and How Do I Manage It?

A bankroll is the cash immediately available to you for a given purpose — in this case, playing poker. It's best to view your poker bankroll as a long-term investment. Do not consider it spendable, stable income such as those funds immediately available to you in your checking account. Your poker bankroll has a purpose and will frequently fluctuate.

In our SNG method, you will start with a $500 investment in PartyPoker. While you are free to withdraw any or all of this money at any time, we advise that you convince yourself this money is tied up and should be accessed only in emergencies. By considering your poker bankroll independent of your day-to-day life, you will disassociate it from the non-poker world. Hopefully, this approach will sever any emotional attachment to the funds, allowing you to view them as nothing more than a tool. The only purpose of your poker bankroll is to invest it in tournaments, gradually building it up until you are earning steadily enough to withdraw funds to your checking account.

The bottom line is that, until you are consistently winning, consider leaving your poker bankroll untouched. Once you have achieved a consistent win rate, determine the amount of money in your poker account that makes you feel most comfortable, and withdraw earnings in excess of that amount every couple of weeks.

Why Play Tournaments (SNGs) Instead of Ring Games?

There are various reasons why we have chosen no-limit SNG tournaments over ring games. Perhaps the most important advantage of tournaments is that they may, in many respects, be considered a science. Their structure allows the player to follow a relatively precise formula to defeat them. Each SNG has the same number of players and follows a structure that remains constant tournament to tournament. As such, most poker variables remain constant and predictable. On the other hand, ring games contain a great deal more variability. Your play requires constant variations based upon the climate of the table. Players are free to come and go as they please in ring games and may buy-in with more funds whenever they like. In tournaments, you are playing with the same players from beginning to end, so you begin to understand how they play. It's much easier, and more profitable, to teach someone how to be a professional SNG player than a professional ring game player.

To be a professional-level ring game player, you must be willing to play at a high limit. It can be very challenging and frustrating to build your bankroll up to the point where you can safely play the higher limits. Contrary to this, SNGs provide you with a smoother progression, allowing you to both learn and earn as you go. The most crucial reason is the fact that SNGs have less bankroll variance than ring games. This means that the financial downswings (a mathematical part of the game) will never be as large as in ring games, so the stress imposed on the player is reduced, and learning is much more enjoyable.

I Got Rivered!
The Likelihood of Losing with the Best Hand

Before embarking on our journey, it's important to achieve the appropriate state of mind. Frustration is the enemy of many poker players, causing them to ignore long-term goals and focus on immediate gratification. Frustration can lead to panic and doubt about one's ability to win. We assure you right now that, if you follow our method of play, you will play winning poker. That being said, we all suffer from downswings, brought about by bad runs of cards, unlucky rivers, or inaccurate player reads. Before you begin playing, you must understand that downswings are an inevitable consequence of playing poker. Our method, however, progresses at a rate such that you will play at levels appropriate to your bankroll. We have designed our system so that you will have less than a 1% chance of ever having to drop back down to the lower levels once you have moved up.

Consider this chapter your written reassurance that you aren't alone in taking those bad beats and that it's all part of the game. The following table examines the mathematical odds of certain hands being beaten by other hands. Our hope is that you learn your pocket aces aren't invincible and losing certain hands isn't as improbable as it may seem. The table illustrates the likelihood of the top 15 hands in poker winning given that you go all-in pre-flop and get called. The first column represents their likelihood of winning against cards someone would typically call with, while the second column represents their likelihood of winning against any two random cards.

Hand Rank	Pre-Flop Hand (s = suited) (o = offsuit)	Win % Against Any Ace or Pairs	Pre-Flop Hand	Win % Against Any Random Hand
1	AA	86.9	AA	85.2
2	KK	71.7	KK	82.4
3	QQ	69.5	QQ	79.9
4	JJ	67.2	JJ	77.5
5	TT	64.8	TT	75.0
6	AKs	63.4	99	72.1
7	99	61.8	88	69.1
8	AKo	61.6	AKs	67.0
9	AQs	60.3	77	66.2
10	88	59.4	AQs	66.2
11	AQo	58.3	AJs	65.4
12	AJs	57.1	AKo	65.3
13	77	56.8	ATs	64.6
14	AJo	54.9	AQo	64.4
15	66o	54.4	AJo	63.6

It's not necessary to have more than a basic understanding of these hand rankings. The take-home point is that pocket aces lose less than 15% of the time. To put that into perspective, it's likely that, out of every 100 times you get them, they will lose 15 times provided you go all-in pre-flop. They may lose 15 times in a row, then win 85 times in a row, or the rate at which they lose may be more distributed. Simply understand that, as long as you are making the mathematically correct moves consistently, you are mathematically guaranteed to win in the long run.

Playing Multiple Tables

We briefly mentioned above playing multiple tables at once. It's crucial now that we go over the importance of learning how to play multiple tables at once and how doing so can increase your earnings.

The tournament method that we describe in this book has been proven over thousands of tournaments. We can provide you with accurate expectations regarding average returns on investment (ROI). For example, you should be able to achieve an approximate ROI of 22% in the $11 ($10 + $1) SNGs. Therefore, for every $10 you put into these tournaments, you can expect to get $2.20 back. So, if you play only one $11 SNG at a time, and it takes you an average of one hour, you are making only $2.20 per hour. On the other hand, if you play four $11 SNGs at a time, you will average $8.80 per hour (4 x $2.20).

Another benefit of playing multiple tables is the reduction of variance. You can easily lose three tournaments in a row. If you are playing one table at a time, that is three hours down the drain. On the other hand, if you are playing four tournaments at a time, you could lose on three of them but come in first on one of them and still make money. Playing multiple tables at once helps to reduce large bankroll fluctuations.

We hope that you can appreciate the value and ultimate

importance of learning how to play multiple tables at once. It may seem daunting at first, but after a few tournaments in Step 1 you'll likely be bored playing only one or two at a time. You should attempt to adapt to playing multiple tables as soon as possible. By the end of Step 1, you should be comfortable playing at least four tables at once.

At PartyPoker, you can play up to 10 tables at a time. To achieve this level of play, you must be confident in your abilities since you will have very little time to act on most tables. You will also need to use software such as MTH or Party Planner or have an efficient two-monitor setup.

The Best Times to Play

The games on PartyPoker can always be beaten, regardless of the time of day. This is especially true for the lower limits. Still, some times are more optimal than others. Games are always easier when you are playing against weak players. The more players on PartyPoker at a given time, the more *weak* players online.

Most poker players used to live in North America. However, due to recent U.S. legislation Americans can no longer play on PartyPoker. Despite this, PartyPoker continues to draw in some of the weakest players online. Over the next few years, we will likely see a dramatic spike in the number of Europeans and, hopefully, East Asians.

Remember, there are still thousands of Canadian SNG players out there. Player numbers used to rise and fall by the North American workday. Now we see a steadier flow of players throughout the day and evening as opposed to dramatic spikes in numbers. The following table can be used as a guide to optimal playing times. All times are expressed in Eastern Standard Time.

	8 p.m.– 1 a.m.	4 p.m.– 8 p.m.	2 a.m.– 5 a.m.	5 a.m.– Noon	Noon– 4 p.m.
Monday	Excellent	Very good	OK	OK	OK
Tuesday	Excellent	Very good	OK	OK	OK
Wednesday	Excellent	Very good	OK	OK	OK
Thursday	Excellent	Very good	OK	OK	Very good
Friday	Excellent	Excellent	OK	OK	Excellent
Saturday	Excellent	Excellent	OK	OK	Excellent
Sunday	Excellent	Excellent	OK	OK	Excellent

As you can see, the weekends are the prime time to play. There are thousands of players, many of whom are unskilled. You shouldn't let this chart completely dictate your playing schedule, but you should understand the importance of playing when the most players are online. This is of greatest importance when playing the higher-limit tournaments. The $109 tournaments and up have a much smaller pool of fish who play them. You should take advantage of them while they are online.

♣ PART TWO ♣
The Journey

You are now ready to begin learning how to win PartyPoker's no-limit SNG tournaments. Each step will provide you with the amount of information necessary to win at the level you are playing. We recommend that you consider as your comfort level whether or not you are ready to progress to the next step. While you shouldn't progress until you have achieved the required bankroll amount, it's vital that you also feel you are ready to move on.

Each step will present you with new, more advanced techniques that cater to the increased skills of your opponents at higher-limit tournaments. Feel free to read ahead of your current step, as many of the more advanced techniques will also be beneficial at the lower limits (they simply aren't necessary to win). Each step is designed to build upon the knowledge acquired in previous steps.

The following short forms and terms will be used frequently throughout this part (please refer to the glossary for explanations of other terms).

> **BB** = big bet (refers to the current big-blind value)
> **EV** = expected value
> **Have Position** = when you "have position" on another player, you are sitting to his left (if he's facing the table). You always act after him, so you know what he did before you act.

ITM = in the money (placing first, second, or third)

Open Raise = you are the first raiser (no one has called or bet ahead of you).

Push = go all-in

ROI = return on investment

s = suited, as in AKs

SB = small blind (refers to the current small-blind value)

UTG = under-the-gun (first person to act, to the right of BB)

If you have purchased and installed Poker Tracker and PAHUD, we recommend that you load and make use of them in *every* tournament you play. While achieving accurate reads of your opponents is not of the utmost importance during the first step, nor will it be discussed, it is beneficial to gain a basic understanding of the software prior to progressing to the other steps.

You may already be familiar with the 2+2 forum (www.two plustwo.com), the most definitive online poker resource. It's home to hundreds of thousands of players and enthusiasts encompassing all skill levels. You don't have to be a member to browse the vast database of knowledge. However, if you wish to post questions on the forum, you must register (which is free). No matter what your query, 2+2 will have an answer. If you post a question, it will probably be answered within the hour. Make this website a favorite, and study it often. Whenever you need clarification regarding anything related to poker (including elements of this book), 2+2 should be the first place you turn to.

Pot Odds versus Implied Odds

As previously mentioned, we assume a basic knowledge of how to play Texas Hold'em. We hope that you have a relatively sound understanding of pot odds and how they apply to the game. Here we will provide a brief overview/review of the concept, along with a more complete explanation of one of the key elements of NL-SNGs: implied odds.

Pot Odds Reviewed

Pot odds represent the difference between skilled poker and gambling. They tell the player whether or not investing money into a pot is profitable in the long run or a losing investment. They help us to answer the most fundamental question in poker: If I make this call, and hit the card I need, will I win enough chips to justify the call? Pot odds consider the likelihood of your hand beating your opponent's hand by the river. They are applied to draws of all types: straight draws, flush draws, inside straight draws, et cetera.

Consider the following example. If you flop a flush draw, the odds that you will make that flush by the river are 1.86:1 against you making your draw. Therefore, to justify calling the turn (according to pot odds), the pot must be at least 1.86 times the bet. If the pot is $100, and the cost to call the turn is $25, then you have the odds to make the call. If the cost is $75, then you wouldn't have the odds to call and should fold.

Not every player abides by these rules all of the time. Don't become overwhelmed by the concept, though it may seem at first both tedious to learn and difficult to execute. Through experience, pot odds calculations will become instinctive. The majority of situations you encounter in no-limit tournaments will be straightforward call or fold situations. It's rare that you will be considering pot odds. Often people will refer to "having the odds to make that call" or "I had so many outs, I had to call." Both of these statements refer to the concept of pot odds. The following chart should provide you with a convenient odds reference for both play and interest.

Remember, this is merely a brief review of the concept. Should you have further interest or need greater clarification, consider doing some research on the Internet or reading a book dedicated to the basics of poker. There are literally hundreds of related resources online.

Outs	Turn and River Still to Come		River Still to Come	
	Odds	Percent	Odds	Percent
20	0.48:1	67.5	1.30:1	43.5
19	0.54:1	65.0	1.42:1	41.3
18	0.60:1	62.4	1.56:1	39.1
17	0.67:1	59.8	1.71:1	37.0
16	0.75:1	57.0	1.88:1	34.8
15 (straight and flush draw)	0.85:1	54.1	2.07:1	32.6
14	0.95:1	51.2	2.29:1	30.4
13	1.08:1	48.1	2.54:1	28.3
12	1.22:1	45.0	2.83:1	26.1
11	1.40:1	41.7	3.18:1	23.9
10	1.60:1	38.4	3.60:1	21.7
9 (flush draw)	1.86:1	35.0	4.11:1	19.6
8 (straight draw)	2.17:1	31.5	4.75:1	17.4
7	2.60:1	27.8	5.57:1	15.2
6	3.15:1	24.1	6.67:1	13.0
5	3.93:1	20.3	8.20:1	10.9
4 (two pair draw)	5.06:1	16.5	10.50:1	8.7
3	7.00:1	12.5	14.33:1	6.5
2	10.90:1	8.4	22.00:1	4.3
1	22.26:1	4.3	45.00:1	2.2

Implied Odds

Implied odds consider the number of chips you expect to win should you make the hand you are calling down.

Consider the following example. You are on the button with A6 suited. There is one caller ahead of you. You decide to limp into the hand. The big blind checks, so there are two other people in the pot. The flop comes K93. You flop the nut flush draw. BB bets out with 100 chips. Your other opponent folds. There are only 60 chips in the pot, so you don't have correct pot odds to call. But BB is a weak-aggressive player whom you have position on (she bets before you do). You are relatively sure that if you hit your flush you'll be able to raise BB all-in, and she will call. As a result, you can consider the pot to be larger than it appears; you can consider it to be all of her chips. So you call the 100 chips. The turn brings your flush card, so you hold the nuts. BB bets 200, and you call. BB bets 500 on the river, you go all-in, and she calls. As a result, you knocked one player out of the tournament and won all of her chips.

This is a simplistic example of how implied odds work. It should be taken not as the correct way to play that particular hand but as a lesson on the importance of implied outcomes.

Here is another example. You are dealt 55. A player ahead of you bets three times the big blind. You have played against this player a lot and know that he raises only AA, KK, or QQ. As a result, you know that, if you call this hand and hit your set (trip fives), you'll be able to get him to go all-in. In other words, if you hit your set, it's *implied* that you'll be able to get an all-in call, thus making it the correct pre-flop call.

This example requires an excellent read of your opponent but helps to illustrate precisely what is being "implied." No-limit poker allows for much deeper consideration of implied odds, as both you and your opponents may bet as much as you want, whenever you want. You should always consider the ultimate outcome of your hand. Never bet so little as to provide your opponents with the correct pot odds to call you with draws, nor call large bets unless you are confident that they will be worthwhile by the river.

All-In Hand Odds

The table below illustrates a variety of common pre-flop all-in situations and the odds of the given hands winning. The figures are approximate and may vary slightly (1–3%) depending on whether or not a hand is suited. Any discrepancies in the percentages where they do not add up to 100% represents the likelihood of a tie.

Pocket pair vs. two over-cards	53% vs. 47%
Higher pocket pair vs. lower pocket pair	81% vs. 17%
High-low (A2) vs. in-between (KJ)	57% vs. 42%
Pocket pair vs. two under-cards	85% vs. 14%

The table below shows the outcome percentages of a variety of common pre-flop all-in situations.

Hand Match-Up	Outcome
AK vs. QQ	QQ wins 57% of the time
AKs vs. QQ	QQ wins 54% of the time
AK vs. AA	AA wins 92% of the time
88 vs. AQs	88 wins 52% of the time
AA vs. KK	AA wins 80% of the time
AQ vs. KQ	AQ wins 70% of the time
AK vs. KK	KK wins 66% of the time

It's not important to memorize these figures. However, you

should note that many hands are not as dominant as you may think. The more you play, the more you will come to appreciate that more important than the mathematical strength of a hand is how that hand is played.

If you would like to examine all-in hand odds further, we recommend that you visit http://www.pokerlistings.com/poker-odds-calculator. It provides you with a free online odds calculator.

Step 1: The $11 (10+1) NL-SNG Tournament

Required Bankroll: $500
Estimated ROI: 20–25%

Speed versus Regular

The following method for beating $11 SNGs can be applied to both Speed and Regular tournaments. During Step 1, we recommend that you try both tournament types, then stick to the one you feel most comfortable with. Before deciding, you should keep in mind the following points.

- Regular tournaments generally last about twice as long as Speed tournaments (65 minutes vs. 35 minutes).
- Regular tournaments have less variance. That is, because you are seeing more hands per level, you can wait for big hands. As a result, you will more consistently make money. However, because you are playing twice as many Speed tournaments per hour, your dollars per hour may be slightly higher in Speeds.
- As a general rule, if you are a more conservative player, start with the Regulars. If you aren't intimidated by the possibility of greater bankroll swings, start with the Speeds.

Rules of the Road

These rules will apply to all future steps.

Rule 1: The 10xBB Rule

For now, keep in mind that, if your chip stack consists of more than 10xBB, never push all-in without a raiser in front of you. Instead, raise the recommended amount. If your chip stack consists of less than 10xBB, go all-in instead of raising. The reasoning behind this will be discussed later.

Rule 2: The 3xBlinds Rule

If your chip stack consists of less than three times the SB+BB, you should go all-in at one point before paying your blinds again.

Levels 1–3

Play the following hands in any position.

Hand	Bet Amount	If Raised to You . . .
AA	3xBB	Reraise or push
KK	3xBB	Push
QQ	3xBB	Push
JJ _ 22	Call	Fold
AK(s)	Call	Fold or push

On the flop, do the following.

- When you hit top pair or better on the flop, never bet less than 75% of the pot.
- If someone raises into you and you have top pair/top kicker or better, go all-in.
- Slow-play only sets or better.
- Fold anything worse than top pair/top kicker to any bet.

Level 4

If you still have 1,500 or more chips, continue playing as in levels 1–3. If you have less than 1,500 chips,

- raise at least 4xBB with no callers to you on either the button or in SB with any pocket pair, any ace, or KQ;
- if anyone pushes over your raise, call.

Level 5 and Up

Abide by the 10xBB rule!

Hand	Bet Amount	If Raised to You . . .	Position
AA _ 77	3xBB or push	Push	Any
AK _ AT	3xBB or push	Push	Any
66 _ 22	Fold or push	Fold	Any
KQ, KJs, QJs, JTs	3xBB or push	Fold	Late

Four Players Left (the Bubble)

Over the course of this book, we will dedicate much space to proper "bubble play" since there is nothing more frustrating or expensive than being knocked out of the tournament on the bubble (one place shy of the money).

At the $11 SNGs, bubble play usually begins at Level 5 (200/400 blinds). At this stage of the game, table position is critical. Your play should be dictated by the number of chips you have.

If you have the smallest stack at the table,

- play extremely aggressively until you are at least evenly stacked with one other player;
- go all-in with any two cards when it is folded to you

in SB, unless the BB is the giant stack (so he could easily call you);
  • on the button, open-push any ace, any pair, KQ, KJ, QJ, JT, 9Ts;
  • UTG push any pair and A7 or better.
If you are evenly stacked with others,
  • play tight poker, and only call an all-in with AA, KK, QQ, JJ, or AK;
  • open-push or open-raise with the above, plus TT, 99, 88, AQ, or AJs.
If you have the largest stack at the table,
  • if you have twice as many chips as every other player at the table, consider open-pushing any two cards from SB and the button;
  • only call all-ins with premium cards;
  • you are nearly guaranteed to be in the money; take advantage of this opportunity by bullying the other players as they try to squeak into the money by waiting for someone else to call your all-ins.

Three Players Left (in the Money)

It's at this point that playing the opponent becomes of utmost importance. We recommend that you experiment with different methods of play at this level. Since you are guaranteed money, you should feel comfortable in trying a variety of techniques. More advanced methods will be taught in the next step.

Here are some points to keep in mind.
  • If you are big stack, play aggressively. Steal blinds from the others as often as possible.
  • Once you have made the money, you should be "playing for first, settling with third."
  • Never underestimate the value of being the first to bet. You can make your opponents guess your cards simply by how you bet them.

Heads-Up (Two Players Left)

Again, further heads-up strategy will be discussed in the upcoming steps. For now, get used to playing someone heads-up. Here are a few tips.

- Call an all-in with any pocket pair, any A6+, KQ, KJ.
- Push all-in with the above, plus KT, QJ, JT.
- Take advantage of how your opponent plays:
    - if he is loose, wait until you have a good hand, then call all-in;
    - if he is tight, bully him by constantly raising his blinds.

Never Give Up: Playing with Almost Zero Chips

We will quickly mention the importance of never accepting defeat during a tournament. Occasionally, you will lose a big all-in early. If you aren't knocked out of the tournament, you may be left with what seems like an impossibly small number of chips (15–100). It's extremely tempting to just immediately push all-in and accept defeat. However, this is always the *incorrect* approach. Never consider a tournament lost until it is. We have witnessed hundreds of comebacks, some from as few as five chips. Just be patient, and push as soon as you have a marginally good hand. If you win, push the next moderately good hand you have. Soon you will have enough chips to play proper poker.

It can certainly feel both tedious and fruitless to play out these tournaments. But remember, learning how to play short stacked is part of the game, and these situations provide you with experience. Also, the more tables you play, the less boring it will be playing out these situations.

Step 2: The $22 (20+2) NL-SNG Tournament

Required Bankroll: $1,000–$1,200
Estimated ROI: 17–22%

Opening Thoughts

You should now be comfortable with PartyPoker's software and tournament structures. Hopefully, you have experimented with both Speed and Regular NL-SNGs and have attained a general understanding of the differences between them.

The $22 SNGs don't pose a much greater challenge. While you will immediately notice that the games *feel* tighter, you will quickly realize that the games are equally as beatable. The following points summarize the greatest differences between the $11 and the $22 SNGs.

- There are many more regulars and multi-tablers at the $22s.
- More players will understand the importance of "the bubble."
- Expect fewer callers pre-flop when you open-raise.

Because there is a moderate increase in skilled players at the $22s, your ROI will decrease. However, because you are investing twice as much money per tournament, your dollars per hour will increase substantially. This will remain true as we progress through all of the steps.

By now, you should be comfortable with the basic strategy required to beat SNGs. Each step we will introduce new elements that build upon previous knowledge. You will soon realize that the way you play your cards is just as important as which cards you play. Play each step as you did the previous step, with the exception of the changes we recommend.

Speed versus Regular

If you experimented with both the Speed and the Regular tournaments in the previous step, you likely noticed that you have the potential to both win and lose more rapidly in the Speeds. That is, your bankroll swings (related to variance) will be much more recognizable when playing the Speeds. This remains true at the $22s, only you'll notice greater fluctuations because you are investing twice as much money. Once again, we emphasize that this is all part of the game. Always measure your down-swings in buy-ins. For example, if you lost $55 at the $11s, that is a five buy-in downswing, equivalent to losing $110 at the $22s. This will help to put variance into perspective.

You'll begin to notice that you have less time to react when playing the Speeds. This is particularly apparent when playing multiple tables. We hope that you have experimented with playing at least four tables at once by now. Do not feel obli-gated to do this, but your bankroll will certainly grow faster the more tables you play. For now, however, play only the number of tables you feel comfortable with — especially when starting a new limit. That being said, you'll have to focus more heavily when playing the Speeds. You won't have time to labor over decisions. During this step, we will introduce methods of *reading* opponents. These techniques will eventually be per-formed effortlessly but may seem overwhelming during your first few tournaments. It's important that you have these tech-niques under your belt before progressing and that you can respond to 95% of situations almost instantly. Remember, the more tournaments you play an hour, the more money you'll make per hour.

Our best advice is to play the tournaments in which you feel most comfortable. If you really enjoyed the Speeds during Step 1, then stick with them. You will begin to inherently under-stand the nuances of the games while appreciating differences between Speed players. If you prefer the Regulars, you should stick with them. Even though you may earn slightly less per hour (fewer tournaments per hour), you'll be confident that your play is never rushed and that you are playing your best.

How to Recognize Regular Players

Simply put, the more tournaments you play, the more players you will recognize. If you are running PAHUD, you will imme-diately know whether or not you have played against a specific player along with the precise number of hands you have played with her.

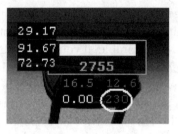

If you aren't using PAHUD, you should pay attention to those players that appear to know what they are doing. As soon as you recognize a player as skilled, make a note on him. This is done by right-clicking on the player's name, then typing in whatever you want. For example, "slow-plays aces" or "multi-tabler." You should learn to abide by the following rule: *Only put notes on skilled players. If you sit at a table with more than three or four notes, consider leaving it and joining another table.* This note-taking technique is advisable even if you are using PAHUD since you generally want to be playing against as many weak players as possible.

How to Play Against Regulars

You should almost always assume that a regular player is a winning player. Most people won't play hundreds of tournaments only to lose money. From this fact alone, you have enough knowledge to take advantage of them at the $22 level. Consider that any winning player has at least the knowledge you obtained from the method described in Step 1. At the $22 level, very few players will have any more knowledge than that. Your greatest advantage over them comes at Level 5 and on "the bubble." Until then, you and the rest of the skilled players are simply preying on the weak players at your table.

Level 5 and Up

Regular players have a much smaller "calling range" than that of weak players. A calling range refers to the number of hands they will call an all-in push with. The priority of a regular player is to make money. She won't call an all-in without cards she is confident are better than yours. At this level, blind stealing becomes important. As a result, if any regular player is in BB while you are in SB, consider pushing almost any two cards, being confident that she probably won't call. Naturally, however, you should use discretion. Don't do this continuously, or she will catch on. Also, follow the 10xBB rule and other tips from Step 1.

THE BUBBLE (FOUR PLAYERS LEFT)

As we just mentioned, the main goal of a regular player is to make money. Since the bubble is one spot out of the money, regular players generally reduce their calling ranges. While it's often prudent to play relatively tight on the bubble (as described in Step 1), you should take advantage of any opportunity to steal blinds. If you are playing against a regular player, you can be certain that he will fold almost every hand to a push.

> • You should push in the SB against a regular in BB with any two cards if you are chip leader and with 85% of cards if you aren't chip leader (see the hand rankings chart in the appendix).
> • If you are on the button with a regular to your left, you can be just as confident that you will steal his blind, thus permitting you to consider your "button-push" more like a "heads-up push."

Playing against regulars will be discussed in much greater detail as the steps progress. The above information, however, should permit you to defeat the $22s with increased ease.

Using PAHUD to Obtain Reads on Players

It's unlikely that you will be able to take full advantage of PAHUD until you have played a couple of hundred tournaments at the $22 level. This is simply because there are so many players at this level, and it will take this long before you have played enough hands with a player to obtain accurate stats. Until then, don't be surprised if only one or two players at your table have statistics.

PAHUD automatically ranks players according to some basic statistics. These rankings are color coded.

RED = skilled/tight player/winning player
ORANGE = average/break-even player
GREEN = loose/gambler/beginner/losing player

The stats appear on your table as follows.

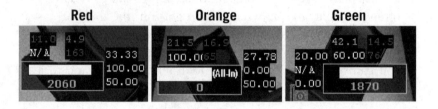

You will notice that only the top two stats change color according to their value. These stats, as you should already know, are "Voluntarily Put $ In Pot (%)" and "PreFlop Raise (%)," and they relate almost directly to the basics of poker. As a result, they can be used to give us an indication of a player's skill level. Your primary gauge of skill level is the "Voluntarily Put $ In Pot (%)" rating (top left). The more a player passively puts money into a pot, the more weak hands he plays. The other stats merely describe the habits of the player.

Consider these general ratings whenever you are involved in a pot with him.

- A red player will only call an all-in with a premium hand, while a green player may call an all-in with garbage just hoping to get lucky.
- A red player understands the importance of the bubble, while a green player probably doesn't even know what the bubble is.

• A red player usually only raises premium hands, while a green player may raise anything.

The key to winning poker is learning how to adapt to other players. The better you are at adapting, the more successful you will be. The $22 SNGs are beatable without being incredibly skilled at player adaptation. Nonetheless, you should take into consideration these basic player ratings in preparation for later steps. By the end of this step, you should have a feel for these three general classes of players and understand the importance of being able to play against all of them.

WHEN TO PLAY WEAKER HANDS EARLY

There is a common debate in the tournament poker world. Most professional players maintain that the best way to be a consistent winner is to play very tight during the first three or four levels of the tournament, then to play very aggressively after that. This is the basic version of the methodology we recommend and have been teaching you thus far. A lesser percentage of players recommend playing very loosely during the first few levels in an attempt to double-up your chips from a weak player who may be knocked out before the later levels. This method is generally not recommended, but it's worth considering. There is a *right time* to play weak hands and attempt to get lucky.

There are certain hands that offer a large reward should you hit your flop. The problem is that you don't want to call these hands unless you know that the pot isn't going to be raised. That is why we refer to these hands as "position hands": we play them only on the button or one off the button. These are the cards we recommend limping into the pot with in Levels 1 and 2.

Hand	Ideal Flop Outcome
Ax suited	Nut flush
KQs, KJs, JTs, T9s, 98s	Flush, straight, straight-flush

Each of these hands provides you with the potential to hit a big flop. In addition, your position gives you betting options should everyone check to you: you could bet and try to steal the pot or check if you hit a draw. The most important thing to remember when limping non-premium cards is to never over-play your hand; never forget *why* you are playing those cards. If you play A2s and hit an ace for top pair, do not play the hand like you are winning it. Never forget that you have a 2-kicker, which is garbage. In most cases, you will lose this pot. If you are going to begin limping drawing-cards in the early levels, you must be willing to fold them if you miss your ideal flop.

Playing weaker hands early is not for everyone. Many people get by just fine without playing this way. This method is best used when playing on a very tight table. Remember to always adapt to your opponents: to beat a tight table, be loose and aggressive; to beat a loose table, be tight and tricky.

Those of you who are playing Speed tournaments should pay particular attention to this section. As you have likely experienced, during Speeds you arrive at Level 5 much more quickly. This means that you find yourself in a position where you are going all-in and stealing blinds more quickly than in the Regulars. As such, you should consider taking advantage of the low early blinds and limping the suggested hands in position. This is because calling a few extra blinds for 120 total chips in the first two levels won't make a great difference once you are in a position where you are constantly going all-in. In other words, because you see fewer hands per level in the Speeds, you should take advantage of cards when you have them, even if they are non-premium hands.

Our hope is that you will experiment with these suggestions. Always treat these chapters as guidelines within which you shape your own playing style. Never feel obligated to make use of all of our tips. You should, however, always attempt to understand the fundamentals behind our recommendations in order to adapt to how different people play the game.

When to Fold Strong Hands on the Bubble

You will occasionally encounter circumstances on the bubble where you may be holding the strongest hand, but the correct move is to fold. This generally occurs when you are one of the smallest stacks at the table. Remember, your number one priority is to get in the money. When a small stack pushes all-in, and someone else calls, you want to fold 99% of the time. It's often extremely tempting to call with hands like AJ or pocket 10s. However, even if you are the favorite pre-flop, there is a good chance you'll lose when you are against two other opponents all the way to the river. This is especially true when you aren't holding a pocket pair but an ace with a medium-sized kicker. As a general rule, never call an all-in (on the bubble) with two or more callers ahead of you unless you have AA, KK, QQ, or AK. If someone is willing to put a player out of the tournament for you, you should always let her. The only exception to this rule comes if you are the chip leader at the table. If you can safely call an all-in, lose, and still have a reasonable number of chips left, then it may be worth the risk to try to kill two birds with one stone. If this is the case, then calling with hands like pocket 10s, JJ, or AQ may be worth the risk.

Remember, this information only applies when someone else has called another player's all-in before you. If someone pushes all-in before you, say SB pushes against your BB, then you must apply your standard poker logic. Consider the player himself: how often has he pushed, how strong a player is he, how many chips does he have left (did he have to push?), et cetera. Again, your number one priority is to make the money. You should never take risks on the bubble.

Strong bubble play is the key to successful poker. You have observed the effectiveness of smart aggression on the bubble — the importance of pushing weak hands when you have to, just to steal the giant blinds and survive another lap. You should always be willing to push with many more hands than you would call with. The reason the push is so effective is because it instills uncertainty in your opponents as you put your tournament on the line. The mathematical property that explains the "edge" you obtain by pushing all-in is referred to as *fold equity*.

Fold Equity

Your "equity" in a hand represents the proportion of the pot that belongs to you. This is determined by the strength of your hand versus your opponent's hand. Consider a situation where you are pushing all-in from the SB against the BB with AA. You know your hand will win about 85% of the time against two random cards (your opponent's cards). If the pot is 1,000 chips, your equity is 850 chips (85% of the pot). This is the number of chips you can expect to win long term, over thousands of hands in this very situation. This is simply "your cards" versus "his cards" to the river. No other influences.

Unfortunately (or fortunately?), poker is not that simple. Because you can vary your betting strategy and playing techniques, you are able to increase the pure "equity" of hands. You should know by now that SNGs aren't as simple as just going all-in when you have AA. More often than not, you are required to push far worse cards. Consider the hand 22. It wins only about 50% of the time against two random cards. If you push this hand on the bubble, you don't want a call. You don't want to put your tournament on the line knowing that in the long run you will be put out in fourth place 50% of the time. But you know it's the right move to push this hand on SB against the BB and try to steal her blinds. What makes this the right move is *fold equity — the chances of winning the pot by causing your opponent to fold*. Once you add the likelihood of your opponent folding to the strength of the hand, it makes it a winning hand.

As always, when you decide to push, you must consider your opponent. *The tighter the player, the smaller the calling range, and thus the greater the fold equity.*

Don't let this concept confuse you. It's not necessary to have more than a slight understanding of equity; don't worry about knowing true values. Simply think, "I have A9, which is a decent hand on the bubble. I think my opponent will fold to a push, so that makes it an even more decent hand. I should win this pot!"

The goal of this section is to help explain (in very simple terms) why aggression increases the strength of your hands. When the blinds are large enough to be worth stealing, it's nice to understand why it is often the right move to push with mediocre cards.

Basic Heads-Up Strategy

Optimal heads-up strategy is highly dependent on the size of the blinds. More often than not, the blinds will at least be at the 200/400 level. If you are playing the Speeds, there's a good chance they will be closer to the 400/800 range. This makes for a 1,200 chip scoop each time you steal both blinds: a significant prize.

The greatest mistake you can make during heads-up play is folding too much. The key to long-term success is aggression. Your opponent's style of heads-up play will become apparent after a few hands. There are generally only two types of heads-up players at the lower buy-in SNGs: tight and aggressive.

If your opponent regularly folds his blinds to you, he's too tight and can easily be exploited. Once the blinds hit 300/600, you should push the top 90% of hands from SB against his BB (see the hand rankings chart in the appendix). Because he folds so often, you should trust his raises from SB and fold your BB most of the time. If he regularly "completes" his SB (he just calls), you should overpush with the top 90% of hands.

If your opponent regularly pushes all-in against your BB, you are playing an aggressive player (obviously!). You should understand that she's playing in much the same way you are. When the blinds reach 400/800 and up, you shouldn't hesitate to call her pushes with Ax, K9+, or any poker pair. You must combat her aggression with your own. When you are in SB, push the top 90% of cards once the blinds get beyond 300/600.

As you can tell, you rarely want to see a flop when you are

playing someone heads-up. The only exception is if you are holding a large pocket pair, such as AA, KK, or QQ. However, because your technique is constant aggression, we recommend that you never alter your betting strategy. If you push almost every hand, you should push the big hands as well. Suddenly calling or making a small raise often sends up a flag to your opponent that you are trying to slow-play him. Keep this in mind when an aggressive player makes this move against you.

It's easiest to understand precisely why this method of heads-up play is successful by examining the "All-In Chart" on page 36. You can see that there are very few all-in situations where you are completely dominated. It's far more likely that you'll be involved in a coin-flip (50/50) all-in such as 55 versus KQ or a 60/40 situation such as A3 versus KJ. The point is that you can't wait around until you get a huge hand such as AA and hope that your opponent pushes all-in or calls your all-in. You must attack opponents aggressively. Remember, fold equity contributes to the legitimacy of your pushes.

There are a couple of additional elements you should consider during basic heads-up play. First, this method should only be applied once the blinds reach a level that makes them worth stealing (300/600 and up). Prior to that, you can play regular poker: calling flops, small raises, et cetera. Try to apply the 10xBB rule when the blinds are lower and scoops aren't necessarily worth the risk. Second, if you are dominating your opponent's chip stack (more than twice as many chips), you should push *any two* cards against your opponent whenever you are in SB or she limps against your BB. Do this over and over, until she either calls or is blinded out. It's worth taking a coin-flip or slightly worse when there's a chance of knocking her out that still leaves you with as many chips as she has.

Step 3: The $33 (30+3) NL-SNG Tournament

Required Bankroll: $1,500–$1,700
Estimated ROI: 15–20%

Opening Thoughts

The $33 SNGs aren't one of the more crucial steps in our journey. The games are only slightly more challenging than the $22s and are beatable with the skills you have already acquired. Our focus in Step 3 will be on "poker moves" or betting strategies that can be applied to specific situations and should be practiced prior to progressing to the higher levels. Most of these strategies will help to establish you as the aggressor in the hand — a position that is always advantageous and necessary for future success. We will also work on fine-tuning your betting in the later levels of tournaments by taking advantage of SNGPT.

Rules of the Road

The 35% Rule: If Betting 35% of Your Stack, Go All-In.

What it is: This is a simple rule that helps you to avoid making a questionable call. Essentially, if you are going to make a bet, and that bet is at least 35% of your stack, then you should just go all-in instead of making the bet.

When to use it: If you are ever involved in a pot as the aggressor (you are the one betting) and you may not have the winning hand.

Why to use it: If you bet into a pot with at least 35% of your chips, then you have made yourself pot-committed. So, if someone raises your 35% bet, you have to call no matter what (unless you have a perfect read on your opponent). As a result, you should bypass this possible situation by simply pushing all-in yourself. Doing so increases the likelihood that your opponent will fold immediately, and should he call you won't be worried about whether or not you made the right decision.

When not to use it: When you are very confident that you have the winning hand (e.g., you are holding the nuts) and you want someone to call you. In this case, you should only bet what you think she will call and try to bait her into putting you all-in.

Tricks of the Trade

RAISING DRAWS

Many fixed-limit players will already know the basics of this maneuver. The method we will discuss applies only when you have position on your opponent. Essentially, if you pick up a strong draw on the flop (nut flush, straight flush, etc.) and one of your opponents bets, you have your three usual options: call, raise, or fold. If you call or fold, you are passively allowing the hand to play itself out. On the other hand, by raising your draw on the flop, you establish yourself as the aggressor in the hand. A strong raise on the flop will result in one of the following outcomes.

		Outcome
Most Likely		Your opponent(s) will call and check to you on the turn.
		Your opponent(s) may fold to the raise, causing you to win the pot immediately.
Least Likely		Your opponent may reraise you, possibly putting you all-in. Here you must consider pot odds, implied odds, and your stack size. If you think you have enough outs (e.g., a straight flush draw), make the call; if you think you aren't pot committed, fold.

Your options for the bottom two results are fairly straightforward. However, if your opponent calls, then checks the turn, you are confronted with further decisions.

If you hit your draw on the turn, you have to consider the type of player you are up against. If you are against an aggressive player, you may bet small in an attempt to show fear that he may have hit *his* draw, thus enticing a reraise from him, at which point you would put him all-in. If he is a tight player, you should bet an amount equivalent to what you bet on the flop. You should think, "If he was willing to call the turn for that much, he may be willing to call the river as well." If you aren't sure what type of player he is, simply bet an amount equivalent to two-thirds of the pot. For now, never check the turn if you hit your draw. When an obvious draw comes on the turn after a position-raised flop, your opponent will immediately fear the draw. It's unlikely that this will change even if you check the turn and allow him to see another card for free. It's better to bet, which forces him to decide whether or not he still has you beat. On the river, you should go all-in if your opponent is pot-committed, or bet appropriately if he isn't.

If you miss your draw on the turn, again you must consider the type of player you are up against. If you know he is tight, you should bet at least two-thirds of the pot and try to win the hand on the turn. If he is loose/weak, consider checking the turn and seeing the river for free. If your draw comes on the river, great. If it doesn't, you invested only a relatively small amount on the flop. You should apply the 35% rule when considering your betting behavior as well.

If you miss your draw on the river, you must consider the size of your chip stack. You shouldn't be obligated to go all-in if you followed the 35% rule on the turn. There is the slight chance that your opponent was on the same draw as you were, so a river bet is optional if it's checked to you. This should be considered when playing with a very passive player, with a high (green) VP$IP in PAHUD. Ultimately, however, all of your river decisions should be made on the turn.

THE STOP-AND-GO

The best way to illustrate this particular maneuver is through an example. You are dealt AK-offsuit in early position. There are six players left in the SNG. You raise 3xBB. The player next to you reraises you to 5xBB. Everyone else folds. So you are heads-up and left to make a decision. You can't fold this hand, so you can either raise her all-in or call. If you call, you become pot-committed, so you have to make your decision now: Do I go all-in here or after the flop? She has position on you, so you are first to act. You decide to call, then go all-in no matter what on the flop (even if you miss). This is the stop-and-go.

This technique provides you with a number of advantages over a simple pre-flop push. If your opponent has reraised you with a low or middle pocket pair such as 77, he won't hesitate to call your all-in pre-flop. However, if you simply call his reraise and the flop comes QJ3, he will have serious reservations about calling an immediate all-in by you post-flop. Essentially, any high card(s) on the flop destroys his pre-flop confidence. Additionally, if he happens to have a huge hand, such as AA or KK, you probably would have lost no matter how you played the hand. You are using the flop as the catalyst of your aggression.

The stop-and-go is best used during the latter stages of a tournament, when hands like AK can't be folded pre-flop and blinds are so large that you find yourself pot-committed after a pre-flop raise. It's also extremely advantageous to use this strategy when you are holding low or middle pocket pairs; as long as an ace doesn't come on the flop, your push will usually win.

Remember, the key to this maneuver is being the first to act post-flop. You can take advantage of this only when your opponent has position over you. There is one exception to this rule, however. That is, when you are in the BB. The stop-and-go is very effective when someone raises your BB, especially when you think she is trying to steal. Instead of overpushing immediately, simply call her steal attempt. Then, when she continuation-bets her initial raise, reraise her all-in regardless of the flop.

THE CALLER SCOOP

This is an effective strategy best used in Levels 3 and 4 when you find yourself in need of chips for the next level. Consider this example. You are dealt AJ on the button. It is Level 4, and you have only 1,200 chips left. Three people limp-in before it's your move. That puts 600 in the pot, plus 100 SB and 200 BB. The pot is 900 chips. You know that someone would have raised AK or a big pocket pair. Your only worry is SB and BB, but you are in need of chips. So you push all-in. That means that, if anyone wants to call, they have to invest 1,000 more chips. Everyone folds, and you win 900 chips without seeing a flop. Now you are sitting comfortably with 2,100 chips.

To use this maneuver, your current tournament situation must meet the following criteria.

- You should be on the button or just one-off the button.
- At least two people must have limped ahead of you (no one raised).
- You must have enough chips that people won't call your all-in but not have so many that you could easily last another lap. Between 5 and 7xBB is ideal.
- You should have a hand that is decent enough to provide you with a fighting chance should you be called — any pocket pair, AK, AQ, AJ, AT, KQ, JTs, T9s. This point is ultimately your decision since you usually don't want a call and should be happy with a steal. More aggressive players will push with *any* two cards should this situation arise.

When to Vary Your Raising Patterns

Until now, you have been getting away with consistently raising AA–QQ 3xBB. Or you may have experimented with alternative raising techniques and found one that better suits your style. Regardless, it's important that we consider when it is appropriate to alter your pre-flop raise technique.

Levels 1–4

You should never be worried about people obtaining reads on your pre-flop raises during the first four levels. While you will run into numerous regular players at the $33s, your goal during the first few levels is to prey on the weak players. As such, never underplay your big pre-flop hands (AA, KK, QQ). Even if the odd regular realizes that you always raise AA 3xBB, the majority of the players won't, and these are the players whom you want calling. Additionally, by consistently raising the same about every time (3xBB), you force other players to put you on a raise range: that is, they must guess what hand you have this time since you always raise 3xBB and you can't always have AA.

Levels 5 and Up

When blind stealing becomes common, you must consider varying your raising patterns. Unlike in Levels 1–4, you will now commonly raise or push with hands that you don't want called in a mere attempt to steal the blinds. This raises a dilemma when you actually get a hand that you *want* called. If you have been pushing regularly, then suddenly raise 3xBB with AA, players will be suspicious. As such, at this level (as in the previous levels), consistency is the key. If you have been pushing regularly, you should push your premium hands as well. Eventually, you'll be called since someone will get fed up. On the other hand, if you have a large chip stack, and have been consistently raising a given amount, continue doing so even when you get a big hand.

Ultimately, you want to leave your opponents guessing. Remember, all-ins usually look like you don't want a call. So never think that you have to suddenly stop pushing simply because you have a big hand. Opponents will be more suspicious of change. In most situations, consistent raising is the key.

It's Time to Start Raising AK Pre-Flop

Many of you may have been confused about why we didn't recommend raising AK pre-flop in the earlier steps. This is because, in the earlier stages, a raise won't prevent many of the weak players from folding out of the pot pre-flop. During the early levels, in the $11s and the $22s, you will still have people cold-calling your raise with JT or other weaker hands. The basic purpose of raising pre-flop is to limit the number of callers and attempt to get a read on those who do call you. In the higher-limit tournaments, you know that people will usually call a raise only with a fairly strong hand (usually a pocket pair or an ace with a high kicker). This allows you to play the flop appropriately even if you don't make your hand. In the lower limits, it's extremely difficult to predict what people will call a pre-flop raise with. If you raise AK pre-flop, and miss the flop, it's difficult to predict whether someone else will hit the flop or not. In the higher limits, because you can loosely predict what your opponents called with pre-flop, you have a better chance of being able to buy the pot with a strong post-fold bet.

At most tables, you should begin raising AK in the same way you would AA–QQ. There are several factors that may alter this technique, however. If there are a number of limpers ahead of you, you should raise more heavily. You should aim for never being against more than three other players post-flop with AK. This helps to reduce the likelihood that someone will hit a flop. Also, you may want to limp AK if your table is extremely tight and often folds around to a pre-flop raise. This is most important in the early levels when the value of the blinds is so low that they are not worth stealing.

If someone raises heavily in front of you, as always evaluate the situation. If no one raises him before it's your turn, you should push. The only hands he could have you dominated with are AA or KK, in which case it's just bad luck. In most cases, you are probably winning — even should you be called. Additionally, he may fold based purely on your raise. If, on the other hand, a player raises heavily, and then someone reraises him all-in prior to your turn, you should fold. It's likely that you are beat.

AK is a very valuable hand, but it's not nearly as obvious to play as other premium hands such as AA or KK. Over time, you'll learn which technique is most effective in a given situation.

How SNGPT Can Perfect Your Game

If you have already downloaded and experimented with SNG Power Tools, you likely understand its purpose: to help you determine whether or not going all-in under certain circumstances is mathematically correct. SNGPT considers your hand, your chip stack, your position, and your opponents' current situations. The software provides mathematical justification for certain poker actions. You may find yourself pushing on the button, getting called, and losing. In these situations, you may wonder whether or not you made the correct play. SNGPT allows you to mimic this situation exactly, then confirms whether or not your push was the right move. Many blind-stealing situations are very clear. You can push with complete confidence, knowing what you are doing is right. However, more ambiguous situations require more thought. SNGPT takes out the guess work, allowing you to memorize what is the right move in that situation.

Here is a screen shot of the layout.

As you can see, you begin by inputting the variables of the tournament itself.

Buy-in	$30+$3 ▼	Hand	
Players	5 ▼	A9o ▼	
Blinds	400/800 A25 ▼	☐ SB Elim.	

Then you describe your opponents.

Position	Chips	Prepost	Bets	All In	Call Range	T	A	L	M
○ BB	2000	20.0% / $60	825	○	66+,ATs+,AJo+	T	A	L	M
○ SB	2000	20.0% / $60	425	○	66+,ATs+,AJo+	T	A	L	M
⊙ BTN	2000	20.0% / $60	25	⊙	66+,ATs+,AJo+	T	A	L	M

The only variable that requires your thought is the "Call Range." It refers to the type of player your opponent is.
• 66+ means he will call with pocket pairs 66 and better.
• ATs+ means he will call with suited aces with a 10 or better kicker.
• AJo+ means he will call with offsuit aces with a jack or better kicker.

You don't have to type these variables each time. Simply click on one of the letters to the right of "Call Range."

Call Range	T	A	L	M
,ATs+,AJo+	T	A	L	M
,ATs+,AJo+	T	A	L	M

T = Tight
A = Aggressive
L = Loose
M = Maniac

Clicking on one of these letters automatically enters a call range appropriate to that type of player.

Call Range	T	A	L	M
TT+,AQs+,AKo	T	A	L	M
66+,ATs+,AJo+	T	A	L	M
44+,A7s+,A9o+,KJs	T	A	L	M
22+,A2s+,A3o+,KTs	T	A	L	M

Naturally, you'll never know your opponent's *exact* call range. However, you should be able to make an accurate hypothesis. If you are using PAHUD, simply apply the displayed stats to SNGPT. You'll be able to tell whether he is tight, aggressive, loose, or a maniac based upon these stats (specifically, "Vol. Put $ In Pot" and "Pre-Flop Raise %"). Alternatively, you probably have a sound understanding of his play simply by having watched him up to that point (and based upon what he called you with).

SNGPT provides you with the following stats after you click "Compute" (obviously, they vary depending on the situation).

EV Fold	19.9% / $59.75	➡	EV Push	23.9% / $71.70	EV Diff.	+4.0% / +$11.94

From the SNGPT tutorial, "EV Fold" is your equity value if you fold the hand. "EV Push" is your equity value if you move all-in, considering all other numbers. The "EV Diff." represents the differences between the two stats. If it's positive, the push is correct. If it's negative, it is incorrect.

You should take some time every day to experiment with the software. Create hypothetical situations and consider their outcomes prior to computing them in SNGPT. Every time you question a decision in play, plug it into SNGPT to determine whether you were correct or not. The more you experiment with the software, the closer you will come to perfecting your game. More than anything else, SNGPT allows you to fine-tune your game to a point where you never lose due to anything but bad luck.

Don't waste your time with simple situations that occur during the early stages of tournaments. Focus on the all-in situations that occur most often. The majority of your time using SNGPT should be dedicated to perfecting your bubble play. Try to practice every difficult situation you can imagine with only four players left.

Under the "Help" menu, you will find a link to the SNGPT tutorial. It will provide you with a complete overview of the software, along with general definitions related to its operation. Further information may be found at http://sitngo-analyzer.com.

Checking Down All-In Calls on the Bubble

As you know, the goal of any good poker player is first and foremost to make it into the money. It's thus mutually beneficial for all players to cooperate when there exists a chance that a player may be eliminated on the bubble. A situation may arise where the short stack at the table goes all-in, and a player ahead of you *just calls*. This is often a signal that he is welcoming another caller to try to put the short stack out of the tournament. If he wanted to go it alone, he would have over-pushed, thus making it necessary for the other two players to call his all-in as well. If you have a decent hand, and enough chips to afford calling the short stack, you should always call. (Alternatively, if you have a huge hand [AA, KK, QQ, AK], you should always overpush. There is a chance the caller may fold, and you will be heads-up with the short stack.) After the flop, you will be heads-up with the other caller, while the short stack is all-in. You should almost always check the pot down with your opponent. He should know to do the same at this level of play. Remember, it's mutually beneficial to have this player out of the tournament.

There are situations, however, where you should not check the pot down with your opponent. If you hit a hand that you are confident is winning, you should bet it or go all-in. Never waste a big hand just to be courteous to your opponent. However, avoid betting with anything less than top pair. You never want to risk tripling-up the short stack.

If you find yourself in a situation where the short stack goes all-in ahead of you, and you are first to act, consider your options. If you just call, you are welcoming other callers. If you overpush, you are sending the message that you want to play them heads-up. It's a good idea to overpush with hands like 99, TT, and JJ. You are probably a strong favorite over the short stack heads-up, so you don't want other players coming along for the ride and decreasing your chances of winning. As per post-flop play, *never waste a good hand*. If short stack pushes to you, and you have a premium hand such as AA or KK, always overpush. You do have the option of calling, and hoping for more callers, but it's not worth the risk of losing on the bubble.

Online Poker Tells: Reads Specific to the Online World

The following tells should be taken generally and applied to opponents who are unknown. There is no substitute for a strong read based upon PAHUD's statistics or your own personal notes. However, these techniques are common among many SNG players and should be understood.

A long delay followed by a check often indicates weakness on the flop. If a player delays for a long time, then checks, she is attempting to imply that she's "thinking about betting." She is usually attempting to deter you from betting so that she can see another card for free. A strong bet will usually buy the pot.

A long delay followed by a bet often indicates strength on the flop. This betting strategy attempts to suggest "hesitation" in betting. Your opponent is attempting to show that he is concerned about betting but is doing so anyway. His hope is to lure you into calling or raising.

An instant check usually represents weakness. An instant check normally suggests that your opponent clicked the "Check/Fold" button. This is particularly true for multi-tablers, who rely on these buttons almost exclusively. So it's often advisable to place a bet against those who exhibit this behavior since they may fold just as instantly as they checked!

A quick check may indicate a strong hand being slow-played. Be wary of any player who quickly checks to you, then calls. She may be slowing down a big hand. If the opponent raises your bet, it almost always signifies a slow-play when done after a quick check. She is hoping that the quick check will be viewed in the same manner as an instant check would. However, you'll always be able to detect the difference between a check based upon a player click and an instant check activated by clicking the "Check/Fold" button. The speed of an instant check is unmistakable.

An instant call after you bet usually indicates a weak hand. If you bet, and are called instantly, it usually means that your opponent has a drawing hand. Be wary of any draws that may come on the turn, and bet accordingly. If the flop doesn't show a draw, an instant call may represent either a slow-play or a strong hand that missed. In the latter case, for example, your opponent may have two over-cards such as AQ and just want to see another card, or he may have a low pocket pair and hope to hit a set on the turn.

Chatting. As a general rule, anyone who chats profusely during a tournament is a weak player. If he has time to chat, he's likely playing only one table and is probably a beginner. Additionally, constant chatting usually suggests that he's just playing to have a good time; his focus is not necessarily on winning.

Some players also attempt to bait their opponents into folding by typing about the strength of their hands. When a player says he has a strong hand, he is generally bluffing.

Step 4: The $55 (50+5) NL-SNG Tournament

Required Bankroll: $2,500–$3,000
Estimated ROI: 10–14%

Opening Thoughts

The $55 SNGs are the "bread and butter" of many online professionals. Games always fill up rapidly, and there appears to be an endless stream of weak players willing to play them. Many people make a decent living playing the $55s. For example, if you were to play 50 tournaments a day, with an ROI of 12%, you would earn $330 per day. If you do this five days a week, you are earning $1,650 per week, *tax free*. This is the equivalent of an $85,000 per year salary that you never have to pay tax on! You can see why so many people play at this level.

The games at the $55s remain fairly soft. You should have no trouble beating them for at least 10–14% ROI. Because there are so many regulars, however, the key to success at this level is being able to exploit their games just as well as you exploit the weak players. The higher the limit, the more important this becomes. In this step, we will continue to examine betting strategies that take advantage of a skilled player's mentality. In addition, we'll show you how to make further use of stats provided by PAHUD (a program you should be taking advantage of by this stage in your poker career). Because there are so many regulars at this limit, you'll begin to amass a much more thorough database in Poker Tracker. The more you play the regulars, the more you will learn about them, and the more accurate PAHUD's stats will be. Eventually, you'll have a perfect statistical profile of your regular opponents, permitting you to make mathematically correct moves almost all of the time.

Additionally, you should study all of your questionable all-in pushes with SNGPT. You should try to perfect your all-in play before progressing to the next step.

Speeds versus Regulars

By now, you have decided which type of tournament you prefer. Here is a quick review of the factors you should consider before making your final decision.

The Regular SNGs have the advantage of allowing you to consider each move more thoroughly. Also, they allow you to more frequently use betting strategies beyond going all-in due to the slower blind progression. If you have the patience for them and find them sufficiently profitable, you should stick with them. In addition, they may allow you to have this book open while playing since you have more time to act.

The Speed SNGs progress more rapidly. Before you know it, you are in a position where you are required to push or fold. Because of this, you must begin to master these maneuvers; consider the all-in push a science, where there is only a right or wrong decision. If you are unwilling to master the all-in, and accept its importance, you should stick to the Regulars (though you should master it for the Regulars as well).

SNGPT is a tool that will prove itself incredibly valuable to the Speed player. Every time you make the wrong push, you are losing money. SNGPT will help you to remain confident that you are making the right move. And confidence is crucial during Speed tournaments, as the swings (both up and down) will be slightly more significant than in the Regulars. You must remain confident that you are playing winning poker. Once you have mastered the Speeds, you will be able to play them more robotically than the Regulars. Less trickery is required to defeat them.

If it were completely up to us, we would recommend that all players play the Speeds. While the swings are slightly more volatile, you'll be rewarded with a higher hourly earning rate. This, to the professional player, is the most important deciding factor. On the other hand, the most important element of poker is that you feel comfortable playing it. Choose what suits your style best, but understand that greater profits can ultimately be had at the Speeds.

Tricks of the Trade

THE AK PUSH

This technique is most effective at the $55 tournaments and beyond. It exploits the tightness that many players have during the early levels of the tournament. Simply, it involves going all-in pre-flop with AK when the time is right. Take the following example into consideration.

You are dealt AKs in Level 3. A player raises 3xBB ahead of you and gets one caller. It is then your turn to act. You could call, but this almost forces you to fold on the flop if you miss. It also puts you in the hand in a state of weakness. Remember, you almost always want to be the aggressor — to have control over the hand. So you consider your situation. The raiser likely has a fairly solid hand. The caller is probably just trying to see the flop, hoping to hit something. Maybe he has a low pocket pair. You shouldn't be concerned about the caller. You decide to push all-in and try to scoop the raise and the call, along with the blinds. This is a total of 750 chips you would win without seeing a flop.

The logic behind this move is as follows. The only two hands that the raiser could have you dominated with are AA or KK. You are betting that he doesn't have one of these two hands. If he does, then it's just unlucky. The other hands he may have are AK, AQ, QQ, JJ, or worse if he is a more aggressive (or weaker) player. If he does have one of these hands, it's extremely likely that he'll fold to an all-in. This is because the majority of players at this level understand basic tournament poker. They are guessing that you are pushing with a very big hand, probably a high pocket pair. Most players won't call an all-in push with AK, because they know that they're 50/50 against any pocket pair, except AA and KK (in which case they are dominated). They won't be willing to put the tournament on the line with a coin-flip during the first three or four levels of play. The same logic applies if the raiser has QQ–22 calling range. They know that, if you have AK, they are 50/50 with you, and they don't want to risk that this early, so they will fold.

A further advantage emerges when we consider the limper: the weak/passive player in the pot. He will almost always fold, but on occasion he will simply be a weak player unable to get away from a mediocre hand. Don't be surprised if he calls your all-in with AQ or AJ.

Finally, even if you do get called, you are at worst 50/50 against any hand he calls with except AA or KK, which is just bad luck.

You are essentially applying reverse logic to this situation. It should go without saying that you don't call an all-in with AK in the first three levels unless you know you are against a weak opponent who goes all-in with AQ, AJ, et cetera. Therefore, you should expect most of your stronger opponents to consider the situation similarly and fold. When playing against regulars, always consider how you would behave in their situations, and apply that logic to your attack against them.

BLUFFING A SCARY FLOP

Now that you are playing more consistently with strong poker players, we can exploit their fears of being beaten by a stronger hand that many weak players wouldn't recognize. One of the greatest differences between skilled and unskilled players is their ability to fold a losing hand even when they have bet into the pot. A winning player always considers the value of calling a hand versus folding and patiently waiting for another. A losing player is commonly impatient and has difficulty folding a hand once he is involved.

This maneuver is almost always performed from the SB or BB and only when you have limped into the pot. By limping into a pot from SB or BB, your opponents can never guess which cards you have. Because it was cheap/free for you to see the flop, you could be holding anything.

The success of this play is dependent on the flop. You need a flop that caters to an SB/BB hand: low cards that no one would play in any other position. The most successful flops include those that have two low cards paired up — flops like 55J, 772, or 33Q. You play your hand as though you are check-raising three-of-a-kind by checking the flop. Inevitably, someone will bet. When it comes back to you, either raise very large or go all-in. This is dependent on your chip stack size. Remember, you *need* your opponents to fold in order to win, but most of them will. A more advanced technique is to simply call their bets with nothing, as though you are slow-playing the trips. Then you either push on the turn or check-raise the turn. Other scary flops include low straight possibilities, such as 679, or flush possibilities.

You can also apply this maneuver when you aren't in the blinds but you miss your flop. For example, if the flop comes JJ9 and someone bets ahead of you, you could raise or push, thus bluffing your jack. You are assuming that your opponent wouldn't bet out with a jack and that he would think it feasible that you played a jack pre-flop.

These bluffs require very specific circumstances but can often help you out of a difficult situation during the later stages of the tournament. You should only attempt these maneuvers if you are in desperate need of chips, have a great abundance of chips, or have a complete read on your opponent(s).

PAHUD's Other Stats and How to Use Them

By now, you have likely accumulated a significant database of players, thus increasing the accuracy of your displayed player statistics. This database permits you to take advantage of more situation-specific stats that PAHUD provides.

It's important to recall that we have configured PAHUD in such a way that players' stats represent how they play within a certain range of levels. We did this when we first set up PAHUD to express certain statistics based upon the number of players at the table (see page 16). As you have learned, people generally play tight early and more loose-aggressive later. You should begin to consider this when interpreting player statistics. For example, expect blind steal attempts to go up as fewer players remain at the table and the levels progress.

Also, you should always look at the number of recorded hands you have on a player when considering the accuracy of your stats.

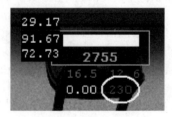

Remember, the more recorded hands you have, the more accurate your stats will be.

CONTINUATION BET (%)
This stat appears on your poker table as follows.

It represents the percentage of time a player will bet the flop following a pre-flop raise. In the example above, the player bets the flop 100% of the time after a pre-flop raise. This is extremely easy to exploit, as you know that she doesn't have AA every time she raises and that she will miss the flop more often than not. Simply consider the most likely hands raised pre-flop, and react accordingly. Depending on the situation, you should almost always raise a player on the flop who has a 100% continuation bet, particularly if you are heads-up with her in the pot. Remember not to get yourself pot-committed and to apply all of your rules when determining bet size.

If a player has a very low continuation bet percentage, say between 10% and 30%, he is providing you with an even more obvious signal. You know that he is only betting the flop when he feels he still has the winning hand after the flop. So you can confidently fold to his continuation bet knowing he has a hand. In addition, if he doesn't bet, you will usually be able to buy the pot immediately by betting the flop (even if you have nothing).

ATTEMPTED TO STEAL (%)
This stat appears on your poker table as follows.

Poker Tracker considers it a steal attempt "if a player raises from the cut-off (one position before the button) or from the button when everyone else in the hand has folded before them." The stat PAHUD provides you with represents the percentage of times the player engages in this behavior. As with the continuation bet, you should pay greatest attention to those players with either a very low (5–15%) or a very high (75–100%) percentage.

Players with low steal attempt percentages are generally very honest players who only raise when they have hands worthy of a steal attempt. You should fold the majority of hands to their raises. On the other hand, because this low percentage implies a lack of aggression, you may consider seeing the flop, then betting it regardless of what appears. Because they are non-aggressive, and relatively tight, they may fold. The stop-and-go, discussed earlier, is another strategy that is often effective in this situation.

Players with high steal attempt percentages are generally very aggressive. They are willing to raise any mediocre hand in an attempt to scoop the blinds. When playing against these players, you should generally attempt to outplay them pre-flop. Because they attempt to steal so often, it's extremely difficult to determine what hands they may be holding. You may be put in a difficult situation on the flop. You should consider putting in a heavy raise overtop of their steal attempt. It's extremely important to bet appropriately. Remember, your goal is to make them fold; you don't want them calling and getting lucky. You should raise at least twice as much as they bet. If you are low on chips, then you should consider the 35% rule and go all-in instead.

When interpreting this statistic, always take into account the continuation bet stat as well. It helps to provide you with an indication of how you may play the flop should you simply call a raise.

A final point to keep in mind is that many players raise any ace (Ax) in the later levels when attempting to steal. If you ever have AJ, AT, A9, or another moderately strong ace, you may want to consider just calling a flop. If an ace comes, your opponent will be unable to get away from the flop. Check to him, let him bet his ace, and then go all-in. This is better than pushing all-in pre-flop since it makes your opponent think you may have anything. This allows you to take advantage of the stop-and-go should you miss the flop.

FOLDED BB AND SB TO A STEAL (%)

This stat appears on your poker table as follows.

As you should know by now, the middle statistic represents SB, while the lower statistic represents BB. These statistics are of greatest importance when blind-stealing becomes a crucial part of the game.

This statistic represents the percentage of times the player folds his hand to a "steal attempt" (defined above). Interpretation of this stat is as follows: a high fold percentage represents a tight player, while a low fold percentage represents a loose and/or aggressive player.

You should be willing to attempt steals with almost any two cards against the very tight players. On the other hand, against very loose players, you should attempt steals only with more premium hands (obviously!).

Player Reads: The Limp Reraise

You may have already encountered this in your journey thus far. A player limps UTG, someone raises, then when it gets back to the player UTG he either reraises or goes all-in. This is known as the "limp reraise" and almost always means that the player has AA (and occasionally KK).

Simply, the player UTG was hoping that someone else would raise so that he could then reraise or push. We never recommend using this technique (unless there are only a few players left and your table is extremely tight). It's not worth taking the risk that five other people limp into the pot and you end up losing when someone hits a bigger flop than you do.

Whenever you observe someone use this maneuver, you should place a note on the player. Should you have someone limp reraise *your* raise, you should proceed with caution. Obviously, you are going to call with AA or KK. However, you should strongly consider folding if you are holding a hand such as AK or QQ. Naturally, a number of factors must go into your ultimate decision: your chip stack, the tournament level, the number of players left, et cetera. But always keep in mind that a limp reraise generally signifies a monster hand.

Keeping the Short Stack Alive on the Bubble
When You Are the Big Stack

This is an advanced technique designed to exploit the tightness of most players on the bubble. It requires the following bubble situation.

- You have at least 1.5 times the chips of the next largest stack.
- Two players have roughly the same number of chips (medium stacks).
- One player has very few chips left, such that he must push every lap just to stay alive.

If you have the largest stack of chips at the table, so that no matter who calls one of your all-ins you'll still be comfortably alive, you have an opportunity to take significant advantage of the two medium stacks. Remember, as always, that their primary goal is to make the money. They won't call an all-in unless they are extremely confident in their cards. They will patiently wait until the short stack is knocked out of the tournament.

Because you have the largest number of chips, they will often rely on you to call the short stack all-in, thus taking a stab at putting her out of the tournament. Many times the short stack may not even have enough chips to double the blinds, thus making it a mathematically *mandatory* call if you are in BB. Nonetheless, keeping this player alive provides you with a massive advantage over the two medium-stacked players, thus making a fold the correct long-term play.

Because you have at least 1.5 times your opponents' chips, and one player is almost out of the tournament, you can safely push *any two cards* against the medium stacks when they are in SB and BB. They can't justify putting the tournament on the line unless they have huge hands. And, even if they do get frustrated and call, you still have a chance to beat them. The worst case scenario is that you end up short stacked, with one player almost out of the tournament anyway — not that bad considering how rarely this happens.

You should be able to scoop thousands of chips off them by the time the short stack finally gets knocked out. This puts you in an incredibly powerful position once you are in the money since your other two opponents will have significantly depleted stacks. You should be able to aggressively hammer their blinds until they crumble, using your giant stack as the catalyst of your aggression.

Remember, in the long term, it's the first-place finishes that provide your bankroll with an added boost. A solid first-place finish percentage makes the difference between moderate and outstanding earnings. Always think ahead of the hand you are playing. If there is an opportunity on the bubble to increase the likelihood of a first-place finish, take advantage of it! Once you are in the money, play for first and settle with third.

Step 5: The $109 (100+9) NL-SNG Tournament

Required Bankroll: $5,000
Estimated ROI: 8–13%

Opening Thoughts

It should now be apparent that terrific profits can be obtained through online poker. The $55 tournaments represented your step into serious poker playing — where the earnings go beyond spare change. You may have noticed that PartyPoker offers a $77 SNG. We have decided to skip this limit since the $55s should provide you with more than enough earning potential to build your bankroll up to the point where you can safely play the $109s.

As with each level, you should be able to defeat the $109s with the skills already obtained in the previous steps. However, if you wish to profit heavily from them, you should add further elements to your game. We will continue to examine advanced betting strategies and player recognition. The higher the limit, the smaller the pool of poor players. We must also consider some basic player psychology that helps us to determine how high-limit regulars react to specific situations.

Studying the Tournament Leader Board

One of the most effective ways to note regular players is to study PartyPoker's tournament leader board. If you haven't already explored this element of PartyPoker, it's accessible under the "News & Info" menu in PartyPoker's lobby.

It's very likely that you'll recognize many of the names on the board as opponents you have played against in the past. You may even have significant stats on many of the players. However, the leader board provides you with information beyond what PAHUD supplies.

To be on the leader board, you must be more than just a skilled, regular player. If you hope to be in the top 20, you must play a very large number of tournaments. Indeed, many players sacrifice quality for quantity in their pursuit of leader board supremacy. The most important thing to note is that most of these players multi-table heavily. They will play at least eight tables at once, and many of them will play 10. This is important because, while they are certainly very skilled players, they will be playing robotically. They won't be paying attention to how you play in any great detail. The greatest advantage of this information is that you know they won't try anything too tricky. Nor will they be able to optimally interpret any moves you may try on them. Many of the maneuvers we have discussed can be used very effectively since they will fold without thinking twice; they have to get back to their other nine tables! We recommend studying the top 20 names on the leader board each week and noting these players whenever you run into them on a table.

There's a good chance, however, that *you* will become a member of the leader board community. The information you have been provided with here should certainly classify you among some of the most informed tournament players online. You should look into the offers PartyPoker provides its leader board players. You can increase your earnings simply by being on it.

Seat Selection

At this level, you will constantly recognize opponents — either from notes or from PAHUD. You will also notice that the games don't fill up as quickly as at the lower levels, so you have time to select an advantageous seat.

Generally speaking, you should always try to sit to the *left* of an opponent on whom you have thorough notes and/or PAHUD statistics. This seating provides you with a significant advantage when the tournament progresses to the point where blind-stealing is crucial to your success. This is particularly true if your opponent is skilled, which is likely the case if you have significant data on the player. The higher the tournament level, the fewer mistakes good players make. It's always frustrating having a skilled player to *your* left. You have to assume that she is almost always making +EV pushes against your blinds, and it's thus very difficult to make the correct call against her push. On the other hand, if you are to her left, you take over this role, challenging her to call your +EV pushes.

Obviously, seat selection doesn't make or break a poker player. Your success will certainly not be limited by sitting in a non-advantageous seat. In addition, there's a good chance that the people on either side of you will no longer be in the tournament by the time you have to start pushing. That being said, you should consider taking advantage of such opportunities when they arise. Even if it helps you to win one extra tournament per 100 it's worth it — especially as the buy-ins increase.

Robotic Poker Players and the Importance of Bet Variation

The robotic poker player has played so many hands, and has such a consistent style of play, that he doesn't even think about an action before making it. He has observed almost every possible poker situation so many times that he can act instinctively. The only inconsistent variable he occasionally must consider is *you* and any unorthodox moves you may make.

You may have noticed that many of your actions and decisions (as related to poker) have become nearly automatic. This is a good thing; it allows you to increase earnings by playing more tables at once and focuses your attention on more specific elements of the game. In particular, it frees up your mind to focus on details you may otherwise miss.

You'll be able to recognize robotic players by how quickly they react. They will almost always pre-click their "buttons" prior to their turn. And they will almost always react as soon as it's their turn. This is by no means a bad thing. You'll probably notice that many of the regulars (players on whom you have numerous stats) play very robotically. There is certainly nothing wrong with it, but purely automatic betting patterns open players up to exploitation.

A robotic player generally uses the keypad when placing bets as opposed to using the "slide bar" that PartyPoker provides. Doing so allows him to enter specific bet amounts without fear of error. It's also much faster. As soon as you see a robotic player raise a pot pre-flop, pay attention to the hand. Make a mental note of how much he raised pre-flop in terms of BB: for example, player 1 raised 3xBB. If you are lucky enough to see which cards he raised with at the end of the hand, note it under "player notes": Level 3, 3xBB JJ. Over several hundred tournaments, you'll begin to amass notes on almost all of the regular players regarding their specific preflop betting patterns. Robotic players play specific cards from specific positions (as do you!), and they often raise a precise amount every time they have a specific hand. Many players overrepresent medium hands, such as JJ or AQs. If you find that a player raises these hands more aggressively than huge hands (AA, KK), then you know you can overpush with hands like AK or QQ.

This brings us to the point where we must suggest that you begin to alter your own, perhaps "robotic," betting patterns. You are probably very comfortable with your raising patterns up to this point, and we don't want to interfere with your success. However, other players will note your raising patterns, and it's best to make it as difficult as possible for them to obtain reads on you. You should begin raising less precisely. Instead of entering specific raise amounts, such as *exactly* 3xBB, consider using ranges such as 2.8–3.2xBB. Don't worry about doing the math during the hand! Just add an extra 26 or 68 or 11 chips to your bet to make it appear as though it wasn't well thought out. It also makes it more difficult for an opponent to track your betting patterns since it makes mental math more difficult. This style of betting often appears very amateurish and will prove beneficial as the number of skilled players increases. You always want your opponents thinking you are worse than you really are!

Advanced Heads-Up Play

You have acquired your own style of heads-up play based upon experience that puts an emphasis on aggression. Most of your heads-up opponents at the higher buy-in SNGs will be extremely aggressive from the SB. They will recognize the importance of fold equity and heads-up position. However, their style of play will rarely be as straightforward as those of players at the lower levels. We recommend that you play very cautiously for the first five to 10 hands against a new heads-up opponent. Remember, you can never gauge an opponent's heads-up play based solely on her performance during the earlier stages of the tournament. You should use the first five to 10 hands to consider the following about your opponent.

Player Action	Potential Read
How often do they raise their SBs?	Provides a general gauge of their aggression.
Limp your SB a few times to see how often they overpush to a limp by you.	If they overpush immediately, they are very aggressive players. If they check rapidly, they may have the "check/fold" button clicked. If they use it, you can exploit them by trying min-raises against their blinds and scooping with little risk.
Do they raise specific amounts or just push every time?	If they raise specific amounts, they are showing conservatism. They may be aggressive but are not willing to put the tournament on the line. They will therefore probably fold from pushes against their BBs. If they push every time, regardless of how many chips they have left, they are playing robotic poker. Call them with Ax, K9+, or any pocket pair.
When they raise, are they always raising the same amount?	If they raise the same amount every time, they are playing fairly robotically. Consider calling techniques that suggest a slow-play by you, such as the stop-and-go.
Do they abide by any of our rules (10xBB, 35%, 3xBlinds)?	Apply this logic when trying to determine the quality of cards they are holding. Many other players follow these rules.

Casual, cautious play during the first few heads-up hands not only provides you with a picture of how your opponent plays but also helps to mask your style of play.

A final opponent trait you should take note of, should it occur, is the min-raise. Some players will constantly put in a min-raise from the SB. This is a poor technique, and we never recommend using it. There are numerous ways to exploit it. You can overpush, use a stop-and-go, or slow-play a big hand if you have one. The only time you should be wary of the heads-up min-raise is when it comes out of the blue. If your opponent has been consistently pushing, or raising heavily, then a min-raise (as always) implies a big hand.

Finally, you should always keep in mind the betting strategies you have already learned. All of them can be applied to heads-up play. They help to break up the monotony of pre-flop pushing and keep your opponent off guard.

Player Reads: Recognizing the Stop-and-Go

As you should already know, the stop-and-go is an extremely powerful tool. Unfortunately, it's also a widely used technique at the high-level tournaments. Hence, it's very important to recognize the stop-and-go when it's used against you.

It's rare that you will see this technique applied until the later levels of a tournament, when people must go all-in based upon blind demands and/or desperation. If you raise during this point of a tournament, and someone merely calls (usually from SB or BB), you should immediately consider the possibility that your opponent is going to attempt a stop-and-go. Pay careful attention to her play after the flop. If she quickly checks or pushes, there's a good chance she is using the stop-and-go. Players often check quickly to erroneously imply that they have nothing (that they missed their flop) when in fact they hit a big flop and are trying to slow-play. A stop-and-go tries to exploit this; the player checks quickly to imply the slow-play. She then confirms the "imaginary slow-play" by pushing as soon as you bet. Players may immediately push if they have very few chips left, knowing that if you bet, their overpushes won't be enough to make you fold. In these situations, you should almost always call with any piece of the flop, including bottom pair or a strong draw. More commonly, the player will have a low pocket pair or an ace high with a low kicker.

The key to recognizing the stop-and-go is paying attention to every move the player makes and to his timing. Many players attempt to take advantage of the stop-and-go on the bubble by exploiting the other players' tightness and desire to just make it into the money. And there's no doubt that this is a very effective technique on the bubble! However, being able to spot the move and take advantage of it is even better.

Player Reads: The Min-Raise

The min-raise is used by players in a variety of situations. One of the most common applications is when the flop reveals a potential draw. Consider a flop that brings two diamonds, thus a potential flush draw. You flop top pair, so you bet 80% of the pot or so. The player to your left immediately raises you the minimum by clicking the "raise" button. This action immediately suggests that he's on a draw. It's unlikely that he would immediately raise a set since he has position on you. He would probably just call and raise you on the turn. Also, if he had a set and wanted to bet it, he'd probably raise more than the minimum because he's scared of the flush draw. He will want to make anyone drawing the flush pay for it. The min-raise represents a compromise for someone on a draw; it may cause you to fold, but if not he still hasn't invested too heavily in the pot. The ultimate goal of this bet, however, is to ensure that, if you do call, you check to him on the turn, allowing him to see the river for free. Along with these factors, you must consider the *player* and how he has behaved previously.

Should this situation arise, it's usually correct to overpush here with top pair or better. It's most likely that he will fold, and you will scoop his bet. If not, you are probably the favorite against his draw.

You'll also notice that people use the min-raise frequently when there are only two people in a pot during the later stages of a tournament. As mentioned previously, it represents a compromise between risk and reward. The players are frightened of becoming pot-committed, yet they want to take a stab at stealing the pot. You should always try to note the speed with which a player applies a raise. Many players think that an extremely fast raise shows confidence in a hand. In SNGs, this is the opposite of the truth. An extremely fast min-raise most commonly represents a weak hand being played too aggressively. Players regularly overestimate the amount of bluffing that takes place when only two people are involved in a pot, and they try to take advantage of it through weak-raising. If you are betting, you probably have something, so you should always consider overpushing. Your only other option should be to fold; calling is almost always incorrect. This situation will likely occur infrequently since, during the latter stages of the SNG, most of your play will be all-in pre-flop. However, it's worth understanding the logic behind the behavior should you encounter it.

Step 6: The $215 (200+15) NL-SNG Tournament

Required Bankroll: $10,000
Estimated ROI: 7–11%

Opening Thoughts

Welcome to the big time. Not long ago this was the highest buy-in tournament that PartyPoker offered. Many skilled players make a living playing the $215s. Earning over $200,000 per year is completely feasible at this level should you choose to play full time. While this limit certainly contains its fair share of pros, it also attracts numerous wealthy fish who keep the games profitable. It's the highest limit at which you can regularly open eight to 10 tables at once at any time of the day.

To be truly successful at this level and beyond, it's increasingly important to acquire a mindset that fully appreciates your new opponents. Certain maneuvers that worked wonderfully on the players at the $55s may send up signals to your opponents at the $215s. Most of your opponents will know how to beat the lower limits and will apply their methods to the higher limits. We will show you how to exploit their "fundamental knowledge of the game" and turn their player reads against them. Many players will apply a "skilled player stereotype" to you and most of the players at the table. We will examine ways to play against the grain, thus inducing calls and impairing their reads. Additionally, we will begin to consider the psychological state of many higher-limit players and how we can take advantage of it.

As a final point, we hope that by now you have fully mastered the "art of pushing" during the later levels of a tournament. It's crucial that you regularly make +EV pushes if you hope to succeed. You have taken full advantage of SNGPT and understand the importance of it as a tool for your success.

The Opposite May Be True:
How Your Skilled Opponents Interpret Your Play

General Interpretations

It's important to reiterate that at *all* limits of SNGs there are extremely bad players; the percentage simply decreases as we progress upward. By now, you should be able to pick out these weaker opponents immediately. If PAHUD doesn't provide you with the required information, observing their first few hands should. These weak opponents can and should be played just as we always have; basic poker skills are enough to defeat them should you be lucky enough to be involved in a hand with them before they are eliminated.

The drastically increased number of skilled players at this limit and above requires us to examine our play against them. We must understand them before we can consistently beat them.

Perhaps the most crucial skill to acquire against these opponents is a sound understanding of how they interpret *our* play. By considering their methods of interpretation, we can alter our play to better induce a desired outcome.

The first point to consider is that most skilled players abide by the general rule of play: tight during the early levels, aggressive during the later ones. This is nothing new; this is how we play and how many of our opponents have played. However, it's important to have this notion at the center of our interpretations. If you are a player who follows this simple strategy (which you are!), you'll immediately be grouped among a specific class of player by your opponents: you understand the basics of tournament play. By virtue of being among this class, you immediately come accompanied by a variety of stereotypes.

1. The hands you play during the first three or four levels will only be premium hands.
2. You won't call an all-in unless you have a premium hand.
3. During the upper levels of the tournament, you understand the importance of pushing to achieve fold equity and are willing to steal blinds with average hands.

These stereotypes are very broad but represent the basic strategy that most winning tournament players follow. So how do you take advantage of these stereotypes? Well, for the first two points, you don't.

1. You *should not* alter your play during the early levels. While everyone expects the skilled player to be tight, there is a reason for it: it's the optimal strategy. It's not during the early levels that tournaments are won. Play as usual and hope for a double-up against a weak player.
2. Again, *do not* alter your calling ranges unless you have a strong read on your opponent (i.e., you are almost certain you know he is pushing a weak hand). Calling an all-in should always be done with confi-

dence — either because you think you know what he is pushing with or because you have a very strong hand.

The third stereotype is exploitable. Once you reach the upper levels of a tournament, where pushing is common, never put a raise in where a push is an option if you are holding a premium hand. Because most players understand the necessity of pushing at this limit, and it's so commonly used, a non-push usually sends up a red flag to your opponents. As we have discussed in previous chapters, one of the keys to being "unreadable" is consistency in betting. Therefore, whenever you are in a position where you would consider a blind steal with any two cards, behave identically with a premium hand such as AA or KK. Suppress the urge to slow-play huge hands since the likelihood of being called is actually higher at this limit, in the upper levels, than it would be if you try to slow it down. You'll find that, because pushing is so common at the higher limits, many opponents will reduce their calling ranges when you are in a position where a steal would commonly be attempted. This is particularly true when you are either in SB or on the button, where stealing most commonly takes place. By overbetting your huge hands, you are hiding their true value.

Consider this idea. At the $33s, a huge bet is usually interpreted literally by most opponents. If you push all-in, most players think you must have a huge hand! In contrast, a push at the $215s is usually interpreted as an overrepresentation of a mediocre hand. Higher-limit players more thoroughly understand the importance of fold equity. They question the legitimacy of a push and adjust their calling ranges accordingly.

As a general rule, when considering how to represent a hand, always consider the obvious first and then adjust accordingly. If you have a huge hand, play it like an average hand would be played at the level and limit you are playing at.

ONLINE-SPECIFIC TACTICS

There are various online-specific betting tactics that are interpreted explicitly by skilled online players. Many of these tactics will relate to ideas discussed in the "Online Tells" section.

A long delay followed by a check often indicates weakness on the flop. Many knowledgeable players consider this a standard online tell. People think that a long delay, prior to a check, represents a weak hand because the player is attempting to represent "thinking about betting" when in fact he wants his opponent to check as well, permitting him to see a free card. Skilled players think that delaying before betting with a strong hand is far too novice a maneuver, so they interpret it as weakness. Additionally, at this level, it is very unlikely there will ever be a check-around after the flop: that is, someone will always take a stab at the pot.

As a result, it's often possible to induce a bluff bet with a strong hand by delaying a long time before checking, allowing your opponent a steal attempt, at which point you can either overpush or call and then bet the turn.

A long delay followed by a bet often indicates strength on the flop. This is the opposite of the above tactic. Many players will pause for a significant amount of time prior to betting in an attempt to mask a strong hand. They believe that the delay represents hesitation in betting. However, many skilled players interpret this as an obvious attempt to lure in a call. You have the opportunity to take advantage of this stereotype by applying reverse logic. If you pick up a draw and wish to semi-bluff, or the flop is "scary" and you wish to attempt a full bluff, consider a significant delay prior to your bet. It will commonly be interpreted as an attempt to bait your opponents into calling or raising your "strong hand," thus encouraging them to fold.

An instant check usually represents weakness. This fact holds particularly true for the multi-tablers. If they instantly check to you, they have likely pre-clicked the "Check/Fold" button and moved on to another table. As you know, you can often put in a small bet against opponents who behave in this manner and win the pot immediately. In addition, you can slow-play a huge hand by taking advantage of the fact that many players interpret the instant check in this manner. If you flop a huge hand, consider clicking the "Check" (not the "Check/Fold") button prior to your turn. Your instant check may help to induce a steal attempt, at which point you can raise or push. This technique is particularly effective heads-up since a quick check often suggests a desire to just get the hand over with.

Chatting. This is a controversial subject in the online poker world. We generally recommend that you never chat, or turn your chat function off. Indeed, chatting in general at this limit usually implies that the player is a beginner. This is simply because a multi-tabler doesn't have time to chat before acting on another table. Still, chatting has been shown to have some advantages. Some players attempt to induce calls by taunting their opponents. Comments such as "Hurry up and call, you fish," or "You are the worst player ever" (and many more explicit versions) are designed to encourage a call. The only problem is that many players at this limit don't have the chat activated. Nonetheless, taunting can be an effective technique. If you push all-in and want a call, it's generally best to say nothing. However, if you push all-in and don't want a call, a quick message can often frighten opponents. As strange as it may seem, it's often best to be completely honest in the chat since that is what your opponents are least expecting. For example, if you push KT and don't want a call, you can type right in the chat "Don't call me, I have nothing," or "Please fold." Players will generally interpret such comments as a desire to be called, thus making them fold.

Chatting is certainly not for everyone. However, if you are playing only a few tables at once, it may be worth experimenting with it. And, as mentioned before, constantly chatting generally suggests a beginner, which may be precisely how you wish to disguise yourself.

Step 7: The $530 (500+30) NL-SNG Tournament

Required Bankroll: $15,000–$20,000
Estimated ROI: 5–9%

Opening Thoughts

This is the pinnacle of PartyPoker's SNG tournament structure. To consistently beat these games, you must take advantage of every mistake an opponent makes, you must use every
poker tool at your disposal, and you must play almost perfectly.
Easy, right?

The $530s fill up very slowly compared with most of the
other limits. If you are hoping to eight-table these games, you'll
be out of luck during any hours other than prime time. In addition, you will rarely find more than four of each type of SNG
open (Regular and Speed). If you wish to play more than four
tables at once, you must mix and match Speeds and Regulars.
This, however, shouldn't be a huge problem since we recommend playing only two tables to start, then moving on to four
once you are more comfortable playing at this level. If you can
consistently beat four $530 tables for more than 8% ROI, you
are ready to play more. Only at that point should you worry
about playing both Speeds and Regulars at the same time.

You'll recognize numerous players from the $215s, and you
should have significant stats on all of your opponents. This is
undoubtedly the key to defeating these games: knowledge of
your opponents. Every push you make must be +EV. To make
+EV pushes, you must know your opponents' calling ranges. To
know their calling ranges, you must know everything about
them.

In this final step, we will examine varied and controversial
methods of obtaining and taking advantage of data on high-
limit opponents. By now, you should already have more than
enough pure poker skill to be successful at any limit.

Taking Advantage of the 2+2 Forum

You have taken the time to browse the vast collection of knowledge contained within the 2+2 forum. You may, in fact, already
be a well-established contributor! Regardless, there are several
ways to take advantage of the forum beyond general poker and
hand advice.

First, you may want to start general topics related to who is the best $530 player. If you get any responses, you should consider private messaging (PM) those who respond and asking whether or not they want to "swap notes" or trade Poker Tracker databases. You'll be surprised by how many people are willing to share information.

Second, each week you should run a search in the forum for the keyword "530" in the "subject." This is done as follows.

Just make sure you search within "One-table Tournaments" and that you have "in subject" clicked.

The results will show only those discussions related to the $530 tournaments within the past week. You should read each discussion, paying particular attention to the forum members who respond. You may recognize some of the names, or slight variation of them, as some of your opponents. In this case, study their responses. How they discuss certain hands will reflect how they play. Take notes on specific styles, and input them into PartyPoker next time you are at a table with them.

Finally, make it a habit to read the "Software" section of the forum. New programs are constantly being released, and you want to take advantage of them as soon as they are available. This is particularly true for software updates related to PAHUD, SNGPT, and Poker Tracker. At the least, the software forum helps to foreshadow the future of online poker tools and therefore the future advantages your opponents may possess.

Poker Prophecy (www.pokerprophecy.com)

Poker Prophecy is a website that specializes in SNG data collection. It tracks millions of tournament hands a day on a variety of different poker sites. As a result, it can provide data on almost *any* player who has ever played a tournament. You simply enter the name of the player, and the data come up. Unfortunately, this service is not free. For Poker Prophecy, you must pay a one-time fee of $39.99. This fee allows you to look up an unlimited number of players. The data provided aren't all-encompassing. Poker Prophecy can't track every tournament played. However, it certainly provides you with an excellent overview of players' success (and therefore their skill levels). The data appear as follows.

Player statistics: (<-- go back)	
Player	
Games played	2283
Wins	801 (35.09%)
Losses	1482 (64.91%)
Average Buy-In	$66.84
Players with better winning percentage	361213
Players with worse winning percentage	698049
$530 Table:	1 wins / 1 losses / 50% wins
$215 Table:	21 wins / 33 losses / 38.89% wins
$200 Table:	0 wins / 2 losses / 0% wins
$109 Table:	245 wins / 363 losses / 40.3% wins
$100 Table:	4 wins / 12 losses / 25% wins
$77 Table:	12 wins / 19 losses / 38.71% wins
$55 Table:	36 wins / 64 losses / 36% wins
$50 Table:	397 wins / 874 losses / 31.24% wins
$33 Table:	1 wins / 0 losses / 100% wins
$30 Table:	1 wins / 0 losses / 100% wins
$20 Table:	0 wins / 4 losses / 0% wins
$11 Table:	0 wins / 1 losses / 0% wins
$10 Table:	0 wins / 4 losses / 0% wins
$6 Table:	1 wins / 1 losses / 50% wins
$5 Table:	0 wins / 2 losses / 0% wins
$0 Table:	82 wins / 102 losses / 44.57% wins
(<-- go back)	

And the percentages roughly represent the following skill levels.

Players Win Percentage **40% or higher**	Player is a **Pro**
Players Win Percentage **35 to 40%**	Player is **Very Good**
Players Win Percentage **30 to 35%**	Player is **Slightly Above Average**
Players Win Percentage **25 to 30%**	Player is **Slightly Below Average**
Players Win Percentage **20 to 25%**	Player is **Below Average**
Players Win Percentage **10 to 20%**	Player is **Way Below Average**
Players Win Percentage **0 to 10%**	Player is a **Fish**

It's important to consider more than just their overall win rates. Pay particular attention to the tournament limits at which they play. A high success rate at the $22s isn't the same as a high success rate at the $215s. Also pay attention to the number of games played. The more games, the more accurate the stats will be. For all the players whom you aren't familiar with, consider looking them up and copying Poker Prophecy's stats into their notes.

It's also important for us to mention that the use of Poker Prophecy *is not permitted* by PartyPoker, which believes that it provides the user with an unfair advantage over opponents. This doesn't mean you aren't able to use it. However, you should adhere to some precautions. You shouldn't visit Poker Prophecy's website while PartyPoker is loaded. Most players who take advantage of Poker Prophecy have another computer open beside the one on which they play poker. For example, they use their laptops to look up player stats while playing poker on their desktops. This way it's impossible for PartyPoker to know you are using Poker Prophecy.

We aren't aware of any players who have had their accounts shut down for using Poker Prophecy. Some players have received e-mails asking them to refrain from using it, with no further action being taken.

Conclusion

The Future of Online Poker

Online poker is in a state of constant evolution. This flux can serve as both a positive and a negative influence on the professional poker player. While an unchanging landscape would permit us to master every facet of the online game, so too would it permit beginners to gradually improve their techniques. Our edge, along with our profits, would thus be reduced.

It's more advisable to think of changes as opportunities. Whenever a major change takes place, embrace it as quickly as possible. These changes can be as minor as an alteration in SNG blind structures or as major as the much publicized U.S. player ban by PartyPoker (and others). Every change offers the skilled player an opportunity to exploit those who adapt more slowly.

Major online poker sites recognize the importance of the professional (or semi-professional) player. We are, in many ways, the bread-and-butter of poker sites. Players who play five or more hours a day, on multiple tables, generate the greatest amount of rake for a site like PartyPoker. However, to keep the pros playing, these sites must continually restock the player pool with beginners — individuals who play for fun instead of profit. Without the fish, good players would have a reduced edge and, therefore, a diminished hourly rate. Remember, the number one reason most professionals play poker is for profit and nothing else. When the earnings no longer justify the time invested, professionals look elsewhere to make a living.

Balancing the number of new and learning players with the ever-growing number of professionals will be the central focus of most future changes. Major sites will look to markets that have yet to be tapped. Currently, most major marketing campaigns have focused on non-English European nations. While this has certainly proven beneficial (as witnessed by Party Poker's increasing share price), most experts agree that the future of online poker (and online gambling in general) lies in East Asia. As China begins to loosen its censorship laws, and embrace pseudo-capitalistic values, it will begin to embrace

Western gaming trends. There has already been a dramatic influx in players from Hong Kong, and there's little doubt that poker will spread to other major Chinese cities over the next several years.

It will become important to keep track of where your opponents are from while playing against them. By moving your mouse over their names (as you probably know), you can quickly discover their countries of origin. Keep track of new players from previously unseen nations. When new players sign up, they often play above their bankrolls. You should take advantage of these players while they still have funds in their accounts (or before they are forced to play at lower limits). In addition, take a look at PartyPoker's parent site, www.partygaming.com, every couple of weeks. Read its press releases, paying greatest attention to its marketing campaigns. You should always stay at least one step ahead of your opponents. If PartyPoker is opening its doors to a particular nation on a given day, mark it and plan on playing on that date, exploiting the high-stakes beginners immediately. Also, pay careful attention to the time zones associated with newly incorporated nations, and play accordingly. If you are going to be a professional, act as such and maximally exploit any edge at your disposal.

Final Thoughts

I'd like to leave you with some final thoughts on the importance of mental toughness when playing poker professionally. By now, you have no doubt experienced both the pleasures of upward variance and the heartbreaks of downswings. The more you play, the more you will experience each. The importance of remaining positive during your downswings can't be emphasized enough. During the learning phase, your initial interest in and enjoyment of the game will help to buffer any more natural emotional reactions to variance. However, the more you play, the more poker will begin to feel like a job. Any excitement you initially had will slowly dissipate. This, unfortunately, is unavoidable. A side effect of any task that has been mastered

94

is boredom. Once poker becomes more of a chore than an exciting new employment opportunity, you'll find that variance takes a greater toll on your emotions. Just as a rude employee may send you over the edge if you're having a bad day at the office, so too can a string of bad cards or a brutal river card.

Should you find yourself being seriously affected by these elements of the game, take some time off. Reevaluate why you're playing and why you began playing. It's a sad truth that not everyone is cut out to be a professional poker player. At the same time, some of the greatest (and/or most profitable) players in the world are degenerate gamblers and miserable human beings. It's crucial to find a middle ground when doing this for a living. As with anything, balance can become crucial. One of the most effective ways to maintain balance is to design a strict work schedule. Stick to it, regardless of your results at the end of the session. Avoid chasing losses. Remember, professional poker isn't a battle, it's a war.

Poker is nothing more than a means to achieve financial stability. If it begins to take over every other aspect of your life, take a break. At the end of the day, all you are doing is accumulating wealth. If you're not willing to enjoy it once in a while, or give something back to those you love, what's the point?

Good luck at the tables.

♥ PART THREE ♥

Review Sheet and Hand Rankings

Review Sheet

Rules	Betting Strategies	Reads
10xBB	Raising draws	The limp reraise
3xBlinds	Stop-and-go	Recognizing the stop-and-go
35% Rule	The caller scoop	The min-raise
	The AK push	
	Bluffing a scary flop	

Hand Rankings

Hand Rank	Hand
1	AA
2	KK
3	AKs
4	QQ
5	AKo
6	JJ

Hand Rank	Hand
7	AQs
8	TT
9	AQo
10	99
11	AJs
12	88

Hand Rank	Hand	
13	ATs	
14	AJo	
15	77	
16	66	**Top 10%**
17	ATo	
18	A9s	
19	55	
20	A8s	
21	KQs	
22	44	
23	A9o	
24	A7s	
25	KJs	
26	A5s	
27	A8o	
28	A6s	
29	A4s	
30	33	
31	KTs	
32	A7o	
33	A3s	
34	KQo	
35	A2s	
36	A5o	
37	A6o	
38	A4o	
39	KJo	
40	QJs	
41	A3o	
42	22	**Top 25%**
43	K9s	
44	A2o	
45	KTo	
46	QTs	
47	K8s	
48	K7s	

Hand Rank	Hand	
49	JTs	
50	K9o	
51	K6s	
52	QJo	
53	Q9s	
54	K5s	
55	K8o	
56	K4s	
57	QTo	
58	K7o	
59	K3s	
60	K2s	
61	Q8s	
62	K6o	
63	J9s	
64	K5o	
65	Q9o	
66	JTo	
67	K4o	
68	Q7s	
69	T9s	
70	Q6s	
71	K3o	
72	J8s	
73	Q5s	
74	K2o	
75	Q8o	
76	Q4s	
77	J9o	
78	Q3s	
79	T8s	
80	J7s	
81	Q7o	
82	Q2s	
83	Q6o	
84	98s	
85	Q5o	**Top 50%**

Hand Rank	Hand
86	J8o
87	T9o
88	J6s
89	T7s
90	J5s
91	Q4o
92	J4s
93	J7o
94	Q3o
95	97s
96	T8o
97	J3s
98	T6s
99	Q2o
100	J2s
101	87s
102	J6o
103	98o
104	T7o
105	96s
106	J5o
107	T5s
108	T4s
109	86s
110	J4o
111	T6o
112	97o
113	T3s
114	76s
115	95s
116	J3o
117	T2s
118	87o
119	85s
120	96o
121	T5o
122	J2o

Hand Rank	Hand
123	75s
124	94s
125	T4o
126	65s
127	86o
128	93s
129	84s
130	95o
131	T3o
132	76o
133	92s
134	74s
135	54s
136	T2o
137	85o
138	64s
139	83s
140	94o
141	75o
142	82s
143	73s
144	93o
145	65o
146	53s
147	63s
148	84o
149	92o
150	43s
151	74o
152	72s **Top 90%**
153	54o
154	64o
155	52s
156	62s
157	83o
158	42s
159	82o

Hand Rank	Hand
160	73o
161	53o
162	63o
163	32s
164	72o

Hand Rank	Hand
165	43o
166	52o
167	62o
168	42o
169	32o **Top 100%**

◆ PART FOUR ◆

Conversion Charts for Other Poker Sites

These tables may be applied directly to the SNG method described. Simply adjust the blind level accordingly.

Poker Stars

Party Level	Stars Level	SB	BB	Ante
1	1	10	20	—
1	2	15	30	—
2	3	25	50	—
3	4	50	100	—
3	5	75	150	—
4	6	100	200	—
4	7	100	200	25
5	8	200	400	25
6	9	300	600	50
7	10	400	800	50
8	11	600	1,200	75
9	12	1,000	2,000	100

Full Tilt

Party Level	Full Tilt Level	SB	BB	Ante
1	1	15	30	—
1	2	20	40	—
1	3	25	50	—
2	4	30	60	—
2	5	40	80	—
3	6	50	100	—
3	7	60	120	—
4	8	80	160	—
4	9	100	200	—
4	10	120	240	—
5	11	150	300	—
6	12	200	400	—
7	13	250	500	—
7	14	300	600	—
8	15	400	800	—

GLOSSARY

Action

1. Opportunity to act. If a player appears not to realize it's his turn, the dealer will say, "Your action, sir."
2. Bets and raises. "If a third heart hits the board and there's a lot of action, you have to assume that somebody has made the flush."

Ante

A small portion of a bet contributed by each player to seed the pot at the beginning of a poker hand. Most hold'em games don't have an ante; they use "blinds" to get initial money into the pot.

All-in

To run out of chips while betting or calling. In table stakes games, a player may not go into his pocket for more money during a hand. If he runs out, a side pot is created in which he has no interest. However, he can still win the pot for which he had the chips. Example: "Poor Bob. He made quads against the big full house, but he was all-in on the second bet."

Backdoor

Catching both the turn and the river cards to make a drawing hand. For instance, suppose you have As-7s. The flop comes Ad-6c-4s. You bet and are called. The turn is the Ts, which everybody checks, and then the river is the Js. You've made a "backdoor" nut flush. See also "runner."

Bad beat

To have a hand that is a large underdog beat a heavily favored hand. It's generally used to imply that the winner of the pot had no business being in the pot at all, and it was the wildest of luck that he managed to catch the one card in the deck that would win the pot. We won't give any examples; you will hear plenty of them during your poker career.

Big blind

The larger of the two blinds typically used in a hold'em game. The big blind is a full first-round bet. See also "blind" and "small blind."

Big slick

A nickname for AK (suited or not). Its origins are unknown (to me, anyway).

Blank

A board card that doesn't seem to affect the standings in the hand. If the flop is As-Jd-Ts, then a turn card of 2h would be considered a blank. On the other hand, the 2s wouldn't be.

Blind

A forced bet (or partial bet) put in by one or more players before any cards are dealt. Typically, blinds are put in by players immediately to the left of the button. See also "live blind."

Board

All the community cards in a hold'em game — the flop, turn, and river cards together. Example: "There wasn't a single heart on the board."

Bot

Short for "robot." In a poker context, a program that plays poker online with no (or minimal) human intervention.

Bottom pair

A pair with the lowest card on the flop. If you have As-6s, and the flop comes Kd-Th-6c, you have flopped bottom pair.

Brick and mortar

A "real" casino or cardroom with a building, tables, dealers, et cetera. This is in contrast to an online poker site.

Bubble

1. The point at which only one player must bust out before all others win some money.
2. The person who was unfortunate enough to finish in that position.

Burn

To discard the top card from the deck, face down. This is done between each betting round before putting out the next community card(s). It's security against any player recognizing or glimpsing the next card to be used on the board.

Button

A white acrylic disk that indicates the (nominal) dealer. Also used to refer to the player on the button. Example: "Oh, the button raised."

Buy

1. As in "buy the pot." To bluff, hoping to "buy" the pot without being called.
2. As in "buy the button." To bet or raise, hoping to make players between you and the button fold, thus allowing you to act last on subsequent betting rounds.

Buy-in

> An amount of money you pay to enter a tournament. Often expressed as two numbers, such as $100 + $9, meaning that it costs $109 to enter the tournament; $100 goes into the prize fund, and $9 goes to the house.

Call

> To put into the pot an amount of money equal to the most recent bet or raise. The term "see" (as in "I'll see that bet") is considered colloquial.

Calling station

> A weak-passive player who calls a lot but doesn't raise or fold much. This is the kind of player you like to have in your game.

Cap

> To put in the last raise permitted on a betting round. This is typically the third or fourth raise. Dealers in California are fond of saying "Capitola" or "Cappuccino."

Case

> The last card of a certain rank in the deck. Example: "The flop came J-8-3; I've got pocket jacks, he's got pocket 8s, and then the case 8 falls on the river, and he beats my full house."

Center pot

> The first pot created during a poker hand, as opposed to one or more "side" pots created if one or more players goes all-in. Also "main pot."

Chat

> Typed conversation that you can have with other players at an online poker site (or any online gathering, for that matter).

Check

1. To not bet, with the option to call or raise later in the betting round. Equivalent to betting zero dollars.
2. Another word for chip, as in poker chip.

Check-raise

To check and then raise when a player behind you bets. Occasionally, you'll hear people say this isn't fair or ethical poker. Piffle. Almost all casinos permit check-raising, and it's an important poker tactic. It is particularly useful in low-limit hold'em, where you need extra strength to narrow the field if you have the best hand.

Chop

An agreement between the two players with blinds to simply take their blinds back rather than play out the hand if nobody calls or raises in front of them.

Clean out

A card that would almost certainly make your hand best. If you are drawing at a straight, but there is a flush draw possible, then the cards that make your straight but also the flush are not clean outs.

Cold call

To call more than one bet in a single action. For instance, suppose the first player to act after the big blind raises. Now any player acting after that must call two bets "cold." This is different from calling a single bet and then calling a subsequent raise.

Come hand

A drawing hand (from the craps term).

Complete hand

A hand that is defined by all five cards — a straight, flush, full house, four of a kind, or straight flush.

Connector

A hold'em starting hand in which the two cards are one apart in rank. Examples: KQs, 76.

Counterfeit

To make your hand less valuable because of board cards that duplicate it. Example: You have 87, and the flop comes 9-T-J, so you have a straight. Now an 8 comes on the turn. This has counterfeited your hand and made it almost worthless.

Crack

To beat a hand — typically a big hand. You hear this term most often applied to pocket aces: "Third time tonight I've had pocket aces cracked."

Cripple

As in "to cripple the deck." Meaning that you have most or all of the cards that somebody would want to have with the current board. If you have pocket kings, and the other two kings flop, you have crippled the deck.

Crying call

A call that you make expecting to lose but feel that you must make anyway because of the pot odds.

Cut-off

The position (or player) who acts one before the button.

Dead money

1. Money contributed to a pot by a player no longer in the pot.
2. A player in a tournament who has no realistic chance of winning.

Dog

Shortened form of "underdog."

Draw

To play a hand that isn't yet good but could become so if the right cards come. Example: "I'm not there yet — I'm drawing." Also used as a noun. Example: "I have to call because I have a good draw."

Drawing dead

Trying to make a hand that, even if made, won't win the pot. If you're drawing to make a flush, and your opponent already has a full house, you are "drawing dead." Of course, this is a bad condition to be in.

Equity

Your "rightful" share of a pot. If the pot contains $80, and you have a 50% chance of winning it, you have $40 equity in the pot. This term is somewhat fanciful since you will win either $80 or $0, but it gives you an idea of how much you can "expect" to win.

Expectation

1. The amount you expect to gain on average if you make a certain play. For instance, suppose you put $10 into a $50 pot to draw at a hand that you'll make 25% of the time, and it will win every time you make it. Three out of four times, you don't make your draw and lose $10 each time for a total of $30. The fourth time you'll make your draw, winning $50. Your total gain over those four average hands is $50 - $30 = $20, an average of $5 per hand. Thus, calling the $10 has a positive expectation of $5.
2. The amount you expect to make at the poker table in a specific time period. Suppose in 100 hours of play you win $527. Then your expectation is $5.27 per hour. Of course, you won't make that exact amount each hour (and some hours you will lose), but it's one measure of your anticipated earnings.

Extra blind

A blind put in by a player just entering the game, returning to the game, or otherwise changing her position at the table. See also "blind" and "post."

Family pot

A pot in which all (or almost all) of the players call before the flop.

Fast-play

To play a hand aggressively, betting and raising as much as possible. Example: "When you flop a set but there's a flush draw possible, you have to play it fast."

Fish

A poor player — one who gives his money away. It's a well-known (though not well-followed) rule among good players not to upset the bad players, because they'll stop having fun and perhaps leave. Thus the phrase "don't tap on the aquarium."

Flop

The first three community cards, put out face up, all together.

Fold equity

The extra value you get from a hand when you force an opponent to fold. That is, if you don't have to see a show-down, your hand has more value than if you do.

Foul

A hand that may not be played for one reason or another. A player with a foul hand may not make any claim on any portion of the pot. Example: "He ended up with three cards after the flop, so the dealer declared his hand foul."

Free card

A turn or river card on which you don't have to call a bet because of play earlier in the hand (or because of your reputation with your opponents). For instance, if you are on the button and raise when you flop a flush draw, your opponents may check to you on the turn. If you make your flush on the turn, you can bet. If you don't get it on the turn, you can check as well, seeing the river card for "free."

Free roll

One player has a shot at winning an entire pot when he is currently tied with another player. For instance, suppose you have Ac-Qc and your opponent has Ad-Qh. The flop is Qs-5c-Tc. You are tied with your opponent right now but are free rolling because you can win the whole pot and your opponent can't. If no club comes, you split the pot with him; if it does come, you win the whole thing.

Gap hand

A starting hand with cards more than one rank apart. For instance, T9 is a one-gap hand. 86 is a two-gap hand.

Gutshot straight

A straight filled "inside." If you have 9s-8s, the flop comes 7c-5h-2d, and the turn is the 6c, you've made your gutshot straight.

Heads-up

A pot that is being contested by only two players. Example: "It was heads-up by the turn."

Hit

As in "the flop hit me," meaning the flop contains cards that help your hand. If you have AK, and the flop comes K-7-2, it hit you.

House

The establishment running the game. Example: "The $2 you put on the button goes to the house."

Implied odds

Pot odds that don't exist at the moment but may be included in your calculations because of bets you expect to win if you hit your hand. For instance, you might call with a flush draw on the turn even though the pot isn't offering you quite 4:1 odds (your chance of making the flush) because you're sure you can win a bet from your opponent on the river if you make your flush.

Jackpot

A special bonus paid to the loser of a hand if he gets a very good hand beaten. In hold'em, the "loser" must typically get aces full or better beaten. In some of the large southern California card clubs, jackpots have gotten over $50,000. Of course, the jackpot is funded with money removed from the game as part of the rake.

Jam

To move all-in in a no-limit (or pot-limit) game.

Kicker

An unpaired card used to determine the better of two near-equivalent hands. For instance, suppose you have AK and your opponent has AQ. If the flop has an ace in it, you both have a pair of aces, but you have a king kicker.

Leak

A weakness in your game that causes you to win less money than you would otherwise.

Limp

To call. Generally, the term refers to pre-flop action. For instance: "He limped in early position with 77."

Live blind

A forced bet put in by one or more players before any cards are dealt. The "live" means those players still have the option of raising when the action gets back around to them.

Live

Cards that aren't duplicated in an opponent's stronger hand. For example, if you have A9 and your opponent has AJ, then your ace is not "live" because making a pair of aces won't do you any good. The nine, however, is live; making a pair of nines gives you the better hand.

Maniac

A player who does a lot of hyper-aggressive raising, betting, and bluffing. A true maniac isn't a good player but is simply doing a lot of gambling. However, a player who occasionally acts like a maniac and confuses his opponents is quite dangerous.

Made hand

A hand to which you're drawing or one good enough that it doesn't need to improve.

Micro-limit

Games so small that they couldn't be profitably dealt in a real cardroom. They exist only at online poker sites. You might arbitrarily call games $.25–.50 and smaller "micro-limit."

Muck

The pile of folded and burned cards in front of the dealer. Example: "His hand hit the muck, so the dealer ruled it folded even though the guy wanted to get his cards back." Also used as a verb. Example: "He didn't have any outs, so he mucked his hand."

No-limit

A version of poker in which a player may bet any amount of chips (up to the number in front of him) whenever it's his turn to act. It's a very different game from limit poker.

Nuts

The best possible hand given the board. If the board is Ks-Jd-Ts-4s-2h, then As-Xs is the nuts. You'll occasionally hear the term applied to the best possible hand of a certain category, even though it isn't the overall nuts. For the above example, somebody with Ah-Qc might say she had the "nut straight."

Offsuit

A hold'em starting hand with two cards of different suits.

One-gap

A hold'em starting hand with two cards two apart in rank. Examples: J9s, 64.

Open-raise

You are the first person to act and do so by raising.

Out

A card that will make your hand win. Normally heard in the plural. Example: "Any spade will make my flush, so I have nine outs."

Outrun

To beat. Example: "Susie outran my set when her flush card hit on the river."

Overcall

To call a bet after one or more players have already called.

Overcard

A card higher than any card on the board. For instance, if

you have AQ and the flop comes J-7-3, you don't have a
pair, but you have two overcards.

Overpair

A pocket pair higher than any card on the flop. If you have
QQ and the flop comes J-8-3, you have an overpair.

Pat

A hand that you make on the flop. For instance, if you
have two spades in your hand and the flop has three
spades, then you've flopped a pat spade flush.

Pay off

To call a bet when the bettor is representing a hand that
you can't beat, but the pot is sufficiently large to justify a
call anyway. Example: "He played it exactly like he made
the flush, but I had top set, so I paid him off."

Play the board

To show down a hand in hold'em when your cards don't
make a hand any better than is shown on the board. For
instance, if you have 22, and the board is 4-4-9-9-A (no
flush possible), then you must "play the board": the best
possible hand you can make doesn't use any of your cards.
Note that, if you play the board, the best you can do is
split the pot with all remaining players.

Pocket

Your unique cards that only you can see. For instance, "He
had pocket sixes" (a pair of sixes), or "I had ace-king in the
pocket."

Pocket pair

A hold'em starting hand with two cards of the same rank,
making a pair. Example: "I had big pocket pairs seven
times in the first hour. What else can you ask for?"

Post

To put in a blind bet, generally required when you first sit down in a cardroom game. You may also be required to post a blind if you change seats at the table in a way that moves you away from the blinds. Example: A player leaves one seat at a table and takes another in such a way that he moves farther from the blinds. He is required to post an extra blind to receive a hand. See also "extra blind."

Pot-committed

A state where you are essentially forced to call the rest of your stack because of the size of the pot and your remaining chips.

Pot-limit

A version of poker in which a player may bet up to the amount of money in the pot whenever it's his turn to act. Like no-limit, this is a very different game from limit poker.

Pot odds

The amount of money in the pot compared to the amount you must put into the pot to continue playing. For example, suppose there is $60 in the pot. Somebody bets $6, so the pot now contains $66. It costs you $6 to call, so your pot odds are 11:1. If your chance of having the best hand is at least 1 out of 12, you should call. Pot odds also apply to draws. For instance, suppose you have a draw to the nut flush with one card left to come. In this case, you are about a 4:1 underdog to make your flush. If it costs you $8 to call the bet, then there must be about $32 in the pot (including the most recent bet) to make your call correct.

Price

The pot odds you are getting for a draw or call. Example: "The pot was laying me a high enough price, so I stayed in with my gutshot straight draw."

Push

> To go all-in.

Put on

> To mentally assign a hand to a player for the purposes of playing out your hand. Example: "He raised on the flop, but I put him on a draw, so I reraised and then bet the turn."

Quads

> Four of a kind.

Ragged

> A flop (or board) that doesn't appear to help anybody very much. A flop that came down Jd-6h-2c would look ragged.

Rainbow

> A flop that contains three different suits, so no flush can be made on the turn. Can also mean a complete five-card board that has no more than two of any suit, so no flush is possible.

Rake

> An amount of money taken out of every pot by the dealer. This is the cardroom's income.

Rank

> The numerical value of a card (as opposed to its suit). For instance, "jack" or "seven."

Rebuy

> An option to buy back into a tournament after you've lost all your chips. Tournaments may offer one or more rebuys or (often) none at all.

Represent

> To play as if you hold a certain hand. For instance, if you

raised before the flop, and then raised again when the flop came ace high, you'd represent at least an ace with a good kicker.

Ring game

A regular poker game as opposed to a tournament. Also referred to as a "live" game since actual money is in play instead of tournament chips.

River

The fifth and final community card, put out face up, by itself. Also known as "fifth street." Metaphors involving the river are some of poker's most treasured clichés. Example: "He drowned in the river."

Rock

A player who plays very tight, not very creatively. He raises only with the best hands. A real rock is fairly predictable. If he raises you on the river, you can throw away just about anything but the nuts.

Runner

Typically said "runner-runner" to describe a hand that was made only by catching the correct cards on both the turn and the river. Example: "He made a runner-runner flush to beat my trips." See also "backdoor."

Satellite

A tournament that doesn't award cash to its winners but a seat (or seats) in a subsequent "target" tournament.

Scare card

A card that may well turn the best hand into trash. If you have Tc-8c and the flop comes Qd-Jd-9s, you almost assuredly have the best hand. However, a turn card of Td would be very scary because it would almost guarantee that you are now beaten.

Second pair

A pair with the second highest card on the flop. If you have As-Ts, and the flop comes Kd-Th-6c, you have flopped second pair. See "top pair."

Sell

As in "sell a hand." In a spread-limit game, this means betting less than the maximum when you have a very strong hand, hoping that players will call, whereas they wouldn't have called a maximum bet.

Semi-bluff

A powerful concept first discussed by David Sklansky. It's a bet or raise that you hope won't be called, but you have some outs if it is.

Set

Three of a kind when you have two of the rank in your hand, and there is one on the board.

Short stack

Few chips compared to the other players at the table. If you have $10 in front of you, and everybody else at the table has over $100, you are playing on a short stack.

Showdown

The point at which all players remaining in the hand turn their cards over and determine who has the best hand.

Side Pot

During a multi-way pot (e.g., three players), one player may be "all-in" while the other players still have chips. A side pot will be created out of the betting that took place *after* the one opponent is all-in. As such, there will be two active pots. One will be awarded to the best hand of all three opponents (including the player who was all-in). The other pot will be awarded to the best hand out of the two players who continued to play the hand.

Slow-play

To play a strong hand weakly so that more players will stay in the pot.

Small blind

The smaller of two blind bets typically used in a hold'em game. Normally, the small blind is one-third to two-thirds of a first-round bet. See also "big blind" and "blind."

Smooth call

To call. Smooth call often implies slow-playing a strong hand. Example: "I flopped the nut flush but just smooth-called when the guy in front of me bet — I didn't want to scare anybody out."

Split pot

A pot that is shared by two or more players because they have equivalent hands.

Spread-limit

A betting structure in which a player may bet any amount in a range on every betting round. A typical spread-limit structure is $2–$6, where a player may bet as little as $2 or as much as $6 on every betting round.

Stop-and-go

A play where you call (rather than reraise) a raise but then come out betting on the next card.

Suited

A hold'em starting hand in which the two cards are the same suit.

Tell

A clue or hint that a player unknowingly gives about the

strength of his hand, his next action, et cetera. May originally be from "telegraph" or the obvious use that he "tells" you what he's going to do before he does it.

Thin

As in "drawing thin." To be drawing to a very few outs, perhaps only one or two.

Tilt

To play wildly or recklessly. A player is said to be "on tilt" if he isn't playing his best, playing too many hands, trying wild bluffs, raising with bad hands, et cetera.

Top pair

A pair with the highest card on the flop. If you have As-Qs, and the flop comes Qd-Th-6c, you have flopped top pair. See "second pair."

Top set

The highest possible trips. Example: You have Tc-Ts, and the flop comes Td-8c-9h. You have flopped top set.

Top two

Two pair, with your two hole cards pairing the two highest cards on the board.

Top and bottom

Two pair, with your two hole cards pairing the highest and lowest cards on the board.

Trips

Three of a kind.

Turn

The fourth community card. Put out face up by itself. Also known as "fourth street."

Under the gun (UTG)

The position of the player who acts first on a betting round. For instance, if you are one to the left of the big blind, you are under the gun before the flop.

Underdog

A person or hand not mathematically favored to win a pot.

Value

As in "value bet." This means that you would actually like your opponents to call your bet (as opposed to a bluff). Generally, it's because you have the best hand.

Variance

A measure of the up-and-down swings your bankroll goes through. Variance isn't necessarily a measure of how well you play. However, the higher your variance, the wider the swings in your bankroll.

Wheel

A straight from ace through five.